DRU
LOVE

Celebrating
30 Years of Publishing
in India

DRUNK ON LOVE

THE LIFE,
VISION AND
SONGS OF

Kabir

VIPUL
RIKHI

HarperCollins *Publishers* India

First published in India by HarperCollins *Publishers* 2023
4th Floor, Tower A, Building No. 10, DLF Cyber City,
DLF Phase II, Gurugram, Haryana – 122002
www.harpercollins.co.in

2 4 6 8 10 9 7 5 3 1

P-ISBN: 978-93-5699-367-9
E-ISBN: 978-93-5699-366-2

Typeset in 10.5/14 Arno Pro at
Manipal Technologies Limited, Manipal

Printed and bound at
Replika Press Pvt. Ltd.

To the singing voice
soaring to the peak of emptiness

and

To all the folk
who sing and become 'Kabir'

Contents

Preface

IT was June 2008. In Kempty village near Mussoorie in Uttarakhand, I heard for the first time in my life Kabir as he is sung in the folk tradition. I was thirty-one years old and I had never heard anything like this before. It was raw, powerful, intense, immersive, absorbing and incredibly moving—an experience that simply blew me away! I had previously heard Kabir sung only by classical singers, particularly Pandit Kumar Gandharva's beautiful compositions. But this was something else altogether. It was as if Kabir himself were standing in the midst of the marketplace, alternately challenging, mocking, inviting and persuading.

> Kabira khada bazaar mein, liye lukaathi haath
> Jo ghar jaare aapna, chalo hamaare saath
>
> Kabir stands in the marketplace
> Flaming torch in hand
> Whoever can burn their house down
> Come, walk with me!

The singer was Prahlad Singh Tipanya, from Malwa, Madhya Pradesh, in central India. I'd never heard of him before. Now he is a huge superstar in the Kabir horizon, both in urban and rural areas, helping produce the same effect among countless people who've never heard Kabir being sung this way before.

I also met Shabnam Virmani, a filmmaker who had just finished producing four musical documentaries around her journeys with Kabir singers. The films blew me away too, as they captured a variety of singers and expressions in different parts of India all the way to Pakistan. Shabnam and I soon became friends, a journey that was then to transform into becoming colleagues at the Kabir Project, co-creating a web archive (called 'Ajab Shahar', a Wondrous City) of this folk music and co-authoring books based around these folk oral traditions.

Needless to say, up among those barren foothills with their bare peaks in summer of 2008, a new world had opened up for me. I started travelling with the Kabir Project team and met many other incredible folk singers and lovers of Kabir in the flesh, each meeting giving rise to a fresh wave of inspiration. I began to enter into the world that the songs were describing through their melodies and their words.

In January of 2012 I moved to Bangalore to officially work with the Kabir Project, a partnership that has lasted a long time. More strikingly and unexpectedly, I began to sing Kabir myself. This way of understanding and internalizing Kabir, through singing, through communing with the songs, through the body, and through community—so different from the way of the intellectual or the scholar (of whom Kabir was always scathingly critical)—is what has led directly to this book. If I can feel and say with confidence that I have some understanding of Kabir, it is because I have heard him and sung him.

Being very much a person of the mind myself, it has been a huge relief for me to enter into another way of being, another dimension, so to speak. Now I am able to utilize my body, my heart *and* my mind to grapple with and present what I have internalized of Kabir's message.

Kabir's message, like Gandhi's, is his life (as well as his poetry). We know very little of the historical facts of Kabir's life with any degree of certainty. Neither history nor biography in the modern sense were very well-developed arts at the time. What we have in their stead are legend, myth, hagiography and anecdote. I take these as an excellent starting point. Like the songs which drew me in, the stories belong to the folk tradition. Kabir's life and poetry, both, have been confidently appropriated by the people, that is, the folk. What we have is a well-established tradition that is a repository of wisdom and knowledge not confined by the bounds of strict logical rationality. (Kabir is also scornful, as we shall see, of the ability of pure reason to grasp deeper truths.)

In September of 2018 I developed and started to perform a show called *Ishq Mastana | Drunk on Love: The Life and Vision of Kabir through Stories and Songs*. This show has morphed directly into this present offering. Having shared and performed this show from my present home state of Goa to places such as Delhi, Bangalore, Hyderabad, Singapore, London, Scotland and more, I can say from experience that the story of Kabir's life, combined with his songs and vision, is something that touches and moves many people in subtle and profound ways.

Given all this, the present book aims to weave together an account of the life of Kabir through the legends associated around him. It is not claimed, of course, that these legends are 'true'. They are shared in the spirit of how Kabir is remembered (and celebrated) by the folk tradition. The legends themselves come in many different versions, with different emphases or slants. I have related these legends in the way that seemed most entertaining and instructive to me personally. I have also chosen to leave out some legends in this present exercise of constructing my own Kabir.

In plain words, the Kabir presented here is a Kabir created over time, by the people of this land. Indeed, this is the only Kabir that we have. There are, of course, various problematic and not-entirely-edifying elements in how any tradition evolves and presents itself. (For instance, the effort to erase the historical Kabir's probable Muslim origin. More on this later.) And yet, there is enough in the tradition that merits attention, appreciation and, indeed, absorption. This is the focus of this book.

Additionally, the book seeks to present in a lucid form some of the core, key concepts that define the Kabir worldview (I have called them 'root-ideas'), quoting and translating his poetry liberally to reinforce the points being made, so that we may have some kind of a systematic outline of his philosophy, if it can be called that. (Philosophy, in the Western sense, falls short of what Kabir tries to convey: anubhav, experience, or darshan, vision or conviction, would be better words, since Kabir always claims to base his assertions on a direct perception of truth.)

The endeavour is to see how the stories and songs and ideas all speak to and reinforce each other, to give us a complete, holistic picture of the phenomenon called Kabir. And so I invite you to plunge into the world of legend, poetry, and deep, subtle ideas based on an intensely personal experience of truth—which is what Kabir had, what he aimed to share, and what he stands for. This journey is shared with you, dear reader, in the same spirit.

1

Who *Is* Kabir?

~

Not, who *was* Kabir.

Kabir is a name that throbs powerfully through the very veins of India. Almost everyone has at least heard of him, if not actually heard his poetry, especially in north, west and central India. He's quoted freely by everyone from spiritual gurus to revolutionaries and social activists. Parents name their sons after Kabir if they come from different religions or if they wish to signal that their progeny (and themselves) are beyond the orthodoxies of religion. Classical singers sing his songs to round off their concerts, and farmers, weavers and artisans in villages double up as folk singers at night, having kept his songs alive for centuries through a vibrant oral tradition. Schoolchildren are taught his verses in school as part of their Hindi classes.

About this last point:

Now, kids being kids, sermonizing is anathema to them, and they respond with parody to poetry that is typically fed to them rather moralistically by grim-faced schoolteachers. Here is an example.

1

Kaal kare so aaj kar, aaj kare so ab
Pal mein parlay hoigi, bahuri karega kab?

Act today, not tomorrow
Act now, not today
Apocalypse comes in a flash!
Too much will be left undone.

I remember this well-known verse of Kabir from my schooldays. It was presented in a deadly dull fashion, as a call to finish and submit your homework in time, for example, or to always be obedient and do your 'duty' as prescribed by the elders. Obviously, kids had come up with their own, mocking answer to this.

Aaj kare so kaal kar, kaal kare so parson
Itni jaldi bhi kya hai, abhi to jeena barson!

Act tomorrow instead of today
Or day after, instead of tomorrow
Why the tearing hurry, brother
There are ages still to live!

It was only in my adult life, revisiting this hackneyed and oft-repeated doha (couplet), mauled so mercilessly and joyously by kids, that I marvelled at its breathtaking beauty—how it describes so concisely the coming of death in an instant, suddenly and unexpectedly, with the most important work of life left undone (we will come back to what this is, according to Kabir).

Thus, woven into the very life-fabric of the country, this fifteenth-century weaver-poet called Kabir has become something more than himself.

What if I were to say that 'Kabir' is not just the name of a person who lived in fifteenth-century Varanasi, by the banks of the river Ganga, who was a weaver by trade and a seeker and a poet by vocation? What if I were to say instead that Kabir is *also* the name of a whole stream of thought, philosophy, poetry and feeling? And further, that Kabir is the name of a whole tradition, flowing uninterrupted for over 500 years, that the people of this country have created for themselves, and have inhabited with inspiration, joy and ease.[1]

What do I mean by this? Kabir was an illiterate man who never wrote himself. He only sang. And his songs have been sung after him for hundreds of years, often without being written down. There is no definitive anthology of the poetry of Kabir. There is not even agreement about which songs 'were written by Kabir' and which have been added later. The same song could be ascribed to Kabir or to another poet, say, Meera or Gorakhnath, in different places or times. There seems to be a never-ending supply of new, undiscovered 'songs of Kabir'. His corpus grows exponentially. Textual sources vary widely, and oral sources are even more 'out of control'. In other words, there is no way to pin down or box in the spirit of Kabir. Kabir is a phenomenon that has transcended mere history or personality.

What has clearly happened is that people have felt free to add to the Kabir canon over the course of the years. And thus new 'Kabir songs' have kept cropping up ever since an amorphous oral canon first took some sort of shape. Scholars have meticulously tried to disentangle the threads, especially in modern times, but perhaps these are threads not meant to be put straight. It is in any case too late. The singers and lovers of Kabir have overtaken the notion of 'Kabir'.

This living tradition of Kabir is not a scholarly tradition. It belongs and has always belonged to the people of India. Kabir himself was scornful of scholars, the pandits and the mullahs, with their Sanskrit and Arabic gobbledygook, and their holy texts, who acted as gatekeepers to the sacred.

And so the oral traditions of Kabir do not bother about questions of 'purity' or 'authenticity' or 'authorship'. Which song is 'his' or 'not his'? When was it 'written'? Is it 'original' or are there 'interpolations'? And so on. Instead, the traditions of song that have sprung up around the poetry of Kabir are bursting with vitality and creativity that are profound, self-renewing and energizing.

Kabir is popularly held to be a saint. (The word 'saint' is used in India in the sense of an enlightened person, not in the sense of an individual canonized by a religious authority.) At the same time, he was an ordinary man, probably married with children, who did artisanal work as a weaver, who did not read or write, and who belonged to a 'lower caste' Muslim family. Given all this, Kabir is not at all a remote figure fit only for reverence. On the contrary, Kabir is a name, an image, a heartbeat, very close to the ordinary people of this land, particularly the poor, the disenfranchised and the lowly placed.

And so people think nothing of adding to the Kabir canon. Indeed, it is a matter of pride. Singers and adherents of Kabir will often proudly exclaim: Ham bhi to Kabir hain! (I too am Kabir!) And indeed, this is a central pivot of Kabir's message: If I can see the truth (in my own body, without the help of scripture or priests), so can you, so can everyone else.

This deeply empowering message has been taken to heart by the ordinary folk of India. Kabir's songs belong to them (and not to any high priest or scholar). They have a deep reverence for Kabir's words and yet they are free to interpret them in their own way, musically, poetically and philosophically. They are indeed free to add their own 'Kabir song' to the mix. (And no one will object.) The tradition gets stronger with each addition, the river swells and burgeons with power with the addition of each new tributary. There are 'Kabir songs' featuring guns, cannons, trains and even ticket collectors! (All delightful anachronisms that add colour to this free-flowing tradition.)

Kabir in Arabic means 'The Great'. It is one of the ninety-nine names of Allah. In the oral traditions of north and central India, practised in the shape of all-day or all-night musical gatherings, called satsangs or jagarans, Kabir comes to stand for a great stream of poetry and thought, which is continuously being added to and subtracted from, which is alive, like a river, and flowing!

There is no need to box ourselves into false and tight dichotomies of 'authentic' or 'inauthentic' Kabir, or whether Kabir was one person or has become many. Truth can be multidimensional, paradoxical, encompassing of all possibilities. Kabir is *both* the name of a historical person who lived in the fifteenth century and of a living oral tradition of songs that have sprung up around his name. Kabir is both long gone and still alive. It is neither one nor the other.

> Haan kahun to hai nahin, na bhi kahyo nahin jaaye
> Haan aur na ke beech mein, mera satguru raha samaaye

> If I say 'yes', it isn't so
> But I also cannot say 'no'
> My true guru is to be found
> In the space between 'yes' and 'no'.

This doha of Kabir points to the vital importance of the subtlety of perception emphasized by Kabir, what he calls 'Jheena' or 'Jheeni'.

The nature of the human mind is to get caught up in dualistic ways of thinking. This is more than ever the case in our ideologically fractured times. What if we were to try to transcend the limiting dualities tying us to our decided positions and dividing us from others? What if we were to come to a more subtle ground, as Kabir urges us to do, and think for a moment beyond our hard positions? Left versus Right. Liberal versus Conservative. Hindu versus Muslim. Rich versus Poor. Upper versus Lower. Local versus Outsider. Male versus Female. Us versus Them. For Kabir, transcending duality, this tussle between the 'yes' and the 'no', between 'right' and 'wrong', is key to the spiritual search. It is not a question of either–or, but of 'both/and', a more holistic understanding of reality. Grasping the finer, the subtler, the more jheena aspects of reality and self can help in this transcendence. It is a more sophisticated mode of thinking.

Before we launch into the legendary life of Kabir in the next chapter, it is good to remember that most of the details of his life come to us through story, myth, hagiography and legend. This, too, is an example of people appropriating a figure unto themselves. The mythic truth embodied in the shape of stories speaks afresh to each succeeding generation.

And so, when we ask 'Who *is* Kabir?', the response is that it is the name of this living tradition of legend, poetry, thought and music, which we shall have the pleasure of delving into presently.

Root-Idea: Jheeni | Subtle

Jheeni, or jheena, means subtle. Two hallmark Kabir bhajans emphasize the idea of the subtle very powerfully, and have therefore become iconic. Curiously, one describes the body, while the other describes the sky.

Or rather, a sound in the sky. Which sky? What sound?

> Koi sunta hai guru gyaani
> Gagan mein aawaaz ho rahi, jheeni jheeni

> A rare and wise guru listens
> The sky reverberates with a sound
> Subtle, so subtle.

This song describes a person in the act of listening. That person pays attention. What was previously unhearable becomes audible. Is this sky a space within oneself? Is this subtle sound a vibration in oneself?

Listening to the 'shabd' (word), or 'naad' (sound) is an important idea in Kabir. Listening itself is a central act ('suno bhai saadho'/ listen fellow seekers, is his typical signature line). In a lesser-known song from the oral traditions in Gujarat, he speaks again of sky and sound, implying the effort to listen.

> Aa ri gagan maan vaaja vaage
> Enu jheenu jheenu ae jhankaaro

> In this sky, an instrument plays
> Its resonance subtle,
> So subtle.

We know from our own experience that we cannot hear softer sounds in the presence of loud noise. The gross drowns out the subtle. The coarse overwhelms the fine. And so we understand that a deeper listening demands quietness. Even the senses perceive more when the mind is quiet. And the experience of sound described here is beyond even the senses.

To access the subtle dimension, one must listen, or look, carefully, attentively. One must be present. One cannot be absent, or forgetful, and yet perceive the subtle. Only a wise one listens. Subtlety demands attention, awareness, presence.

The second hallmark song to use the idea of subtle in an iconic fashion is 'Chadariya Jheeni'.

Chadariya jheeni re jheeni
Raam naam ras beeni chadariya

Such a fine, fine cloth
Woven with the essence of Raam's name.

This is a song that is sung in many regions and traditions, in different ways. And yet, everybody knows that Kabir is speaking of the body here, as a subtle and fine cloth. It's a curious idea because the body is usually thought of as gross. But clearly Kabir's idea of 'body' is very different from our exclusively physical one. It includes the idea of 'self'.

The poem goes on to describe all that happens to this subtle body-cloth—it takes nine months to weave, it is pounded and made clean by the washerman, dyed in a wonderful colour by the dyer, but is then worn by fools, and dirtied and soiled. The fineness of the garment seems to call for great care by the wearer.

If the body is the site of knowledge—as Kabir claims in several other songs—and if the body itself contains the sky, then it is not so curious that the body is described as subtle. It is perhaps our minds that are gross! (This would hang well with Kabir's penchant for reversals—ulat!)

In a set of saakhis or couplets, Kabir describes beautifully the difference between grosser and subtler kinds of attachment.

> Moti maya sab taje, jheeni taje na koi
> Peer paigambar auliya, jheeni sab ko khaaye

> All renounce grosser illusions
> No one gives up the subtle ones
> The subtle delusion devours
> Gurus, prophets and holy men.

> Jheeni maya jin taje, moti gayi bilaaye
> Kahe Kabir ta daas ke, sab dukh gaye hiraaye

> For one who gives up subtle attachments
> The gross fall off by themselves
> Kabir says for such a seeker
> All sorrows come to an end.

It is difficult enough to give up anything. One starts by giving up the obvious, which is already a big undertaking. It is more difficult to give up the subtle ego involved in the act of giving up. And still more difficult to give up the even subtler ego involved in the very observation of this ('Oh, how wise and perceptive I am!'). Subtler and subtler forms of self-inflation and self-importance. The Buddhists call this the self-cherishing mind.

The idea of refinement—becoming more fine—enters into this. As our mind stills and perfects itself, the taste of our being becomes subtler, more clarified. Kabir uses many household images to signal this journey of awareness from the gross to the subtle. A common one is that of milk that is churned to make butter, which further refines to become ghee—the clarified essence where things become 'clear', and we 'see'. Another image he uses is that of sugarcane, that becomes jaggery, then gross sugar, and eventually 'jheeni khaand' or 'mishri' or the crystalline form of sugar. It's significant that all these materials need grinding, churning, thrashing in order to refine to the next level of awareness. Inner growth is not without its share of work, effort and a certain amount of pain.

More images from Kabir's poetry speak of an experience/ intuition/perception beyond the obvious. Kabir lives in a jheena land ('des') that he describes as being without sun or moon, wind or water, earth or sky. Sometimes he speaks of his home as being on the tip of a thorn. At other times, on the peak of a mountain, on the path to which even an ant's foot slips. He claims that he finds his rest at a place sharper than a razor's edge. He has moved beyond the realm of the obvious, and made friends with the subtle or hidden. There is a subtlety to this truth, which is profound in its significance.

Paani se bhi paatla, dhuen se bhi jheen
Pavan se utaavla, dost Kabira keenh

Thinner than water
Subtler than smoke
Faster than wind
Kabir made friends with it.

2

The Miracle of Birth

~

THIS story begins as all others with birth. Birth is an elemental fact of life but even this simple fact can sometimes be shrouded in mystery. While Kabir's followers ascribe an unusually long life span to him of 120 years, from 1398 to 1518 CE, more 'reasonable' scholars are divided over whether he lived from 1398 to 1448, or from 1440 to 1518.

The manner of Kabir's entry into the world has inspired many different theories over the years. Let me share three different versions about Kabir's birth, and you can pick the one that you like best.

The Legends of Birth

Version One

Kabir was born to a Brahmin widow (in some versions, as the result of a boon given by a sage—an immaculate conception!), who abandoned the child near a lake called Lahartara in Varanasi. The baby was found and adopted by a childless Muslim weaver couple called Niru and Nima and was brought up by them as their own child.

Version Two

This is the most colourful version and my personal favourite.

Kabir came down from the heavens in a great and splendorous ray of light, descending from the sky to the waters of the Lahartara lake with universal fanfare and celebration. The baby landed softly on the petals of a lotus ready to receive him in the lake. The divine child was found later by a Muslim weaver couple called Niru and Nima, who brought him up as their own child.

Version Three

Kabir was born to a Muslim weaver couple called Niru and Nima (in the regular way, like most children, delivery following upon conception and gestation). Of course they brought him up like their own child because he *was* their own child!

The last one is the most boring version but the most likely to be true. Kabir sings of Raam, Hari and Govind a lot though he clarifies several times that he means the same thing by 'Raam' and 'Rahim', or 'Keshav' and 'Karim'. This makes him especially dear to Hindu followers and a bit of an outcast to more orthodox Muslims. It might have been hard to accept that one who sings so passionately of Raam and Hari might not have been born Hindu at all. It might also have been difficult to accept, given well-entrenched social prejudices, that such words of wisdom, as Kabir utters often, could flow from the mouth of a 'low-caste', illiterate weaver who couldn't even read or write.

And so the figure of the 'Brahmin widow' enters the picture to fix both the 'flaws' in the story of Kabir—he is *actually* an upper-caste Hindu by birth, even though he grew up as a low-caste Muslim weaver. Be that as it may, the ambiguity around his birth (whether he was Hindu or Muslim, or in a way, both) is at least of great comfort to the greater community of Kabir followers and also ties in neatly with Kabir's own views on this matter.

It is hard to say exactly what must have happened since, to put it simply, we do not know. The story of the widow might be true. Or it may not. However that may be, we do have Kabir's own clear, incisive words and opinion in regard to this. So let's listen to what Kabir himself has to say about his genealogy.

Kabir is hardly interested in hiding his low-caste or illiterate status. In fact, he makes proclamations about both with great confidence and panache.

> Tahaan jaao jahaan paat paatambar, agar chandan ghas
> deena
> Aaye hamaare kya karoge, ham to jaat kameena

> Go where there are silk cloths
> Incense, sandalwood and the like.
> Why do you come to my door
> I who am of low, base caste?

About not being able to read or write, Kabir is especially forthright, since he's convinced that the knowledge that is really worth having is not to be found in books anyway.

> Masi kaagad chhuo nahin, kalam gahyo nahin haath
> Chaar jugaan ra mahaatm, Kabir mukh se janaai baat

> Never touched ink or paper
> Never held a pen in hand

The wisdom of all four ages
Kabir proclaimed with his tongue.

And so we see that Kabir makes a virtue of instruments of societal oppression or treats such categories with disdain. This is a hugely empowering attitude, which millions of people who sing, quote and read him have found of great comfort and solace, perhaps suffering from and/or fighting these attitudes that prevail till today.

About the question of religion, Kabir takes a very straightforward position that he belongs to neither.

Hindu kaho to hoon nahin, Musalmaan bhi naahin
Gaibi donon deen mein, khelun donon maanhi

If you call me a Hindu, I'm not
But I'm not a Muslim either
The essence is in both
And I play in both.

Kabir signals an essential freedom of being, beyond the confines and orthodoxies of established religion. He does not want his identity to be fixed. He remains elusive, hard to pin down. He's free to attack the foolishness and hypocrisies of both religions.

There is a kind of conception that has sprung up over time that Kabir was a 'great unifier', that he was some kind of apostle of 'Hindu–Muslim unity'. Kabir would have scoffed at such a suggestion. He attacked both Hindu pandits and Muslim mullahs relentlessly and made a few fair enemies in his time. The unity that he does talk about is of a much higher order than a tepid kind of 'social brotherhood'.

Raam Rahima ek hai, mat samjho koi do
Andar taati bharam ki, ja se soojhe do

Raam Rahima ek hai, aur Kaaba Kashi ek
Maida ek pakvaan bahu, baith Kabira dekh

Raam and Rahim are one
Don't think of them as two
There is a veil of delusion within
Which makes them appear two.

Raam and Rahim are one
Mecca and Varanasi are the same
One grain, many dishes
Kabir watches in wonder.

The unity that Kabir is signalling is beyond the limits of orthodox religion. And till this reality is grasped as a living experience (Kabir 'watches' it himself, he doesn't rely on scripture or a quoted authority), any attempts at achieving a superficial social harmony are bound to end in failure. You need to have an actual taste of this dish to bring about real and lasting social unity.

Kaaba phir Kashi bhaya, aur Raam hi bhaya Rahim
Mot choon maida bhaya, aur baith Kabira jeem

Mecca is Varanasi again
And Raam has become Rahim
The coarse grain has been ground fine
Kabir eats with relish.

This fine, jheena flavour, tasted for oneself, is what brings about real unity and harmony, not 'messages' of universal brotherhood.

Speaking of birth and life, the folk version of one of Kabir's most famous songs, 'Chaadar Jheeni' (The Subtle Cloth), describes the story of human life, from birth (and before birth) till death.

This cloth, says Kabir, made up of the divine fabric (Raam ras), is woven on the spinning wheel of the eight lotuses. It is constituted of the five elements (earth, water, fire, air and ether) and the three gunas (sattva, rajas, tamas). (The reference to eight lotuses can also be taken to mean the chakras.) The entire created world ('prakriti') in Sankhya and Yogic philosophy is comprised of these five elements and three gunas. The cloth is woven on this loom.

Karma is the thread from which it is spun out by the self, and which keeps it going, birth after birth. It takes nine solar months or ten lunar months to weave. In-breath and out-breath are the warp and the weft. When it is woven it is incredibly light and beautiful.

Once ready, the cloth is given to the washerman, who washes it in the pool of the Word and beats it on the stone of awareness to make it pure and clean. It is then passed on to the dyer, who puts fast the colour of the beloved as the base. But on top of it, the cloth is given many different colours and hues, an incredible diversity and riot of colour, which creates all the visible variety of the world.

Many seekers since many ages—a way to say all human beings—have worn this cloth. But no one really knows the art of wearing it. They all wear it and make it dirty. There are blotches and stains on the cloth, disfiguring it.

Yet there have been a few, a rare few, who have known how to wear it. Traditional mythological icons of devotion like Dhruv and Prahlad, or later-day saints Peepa Das and Sukhdev, wore it and kept it clean. Kabir says that he himself wore it with great care, attention and skill, and he returned it just as he had received it, clean, pure and unblemished. Jyon ki tyon. As it was.

This incredible, fine cloth, the human being, made of the nectar of Raam. But who or what is Raam?

Root-Idea: 'Raam'

What is the meaning or significance of Raam (also spelt 'Ram' or 'Rama') for Kabir? When he invokes Raam repeatedly, what is he really invoking?

In Hindu mythology, Raam is one of the avatars of Vishnu, like Krishna. He is the eldest son of Dashrath, king of Ayodhya. The whole of the epic Ramayana is based on his life. He is a widely revered deity, worshipped along with his wife Sita and younger brother Lakshman. He stands for moral uprightness and rectitude in his life and conduct.

Kabir's Raam is different.

> Ek Raam Dashrath ka beta, dooja ghat ghat mein baitha
> Teeje Raam ka sakal pasaara, chautha sabhi se nyaara

> There is one Raam, who was son of Dashrath
> The second Raam is in every body
> The third is in every inch of space
> And the fourth is beyond even these.

As becomes obvious very quickly, Kabir is not talking about the mythological Raam, now worshipped as a 'sagun' deity, that is, in the form of an idol established in a temple. ('Sagun' means with qualities or attributes, that is, with a definite form; 'Nirgun' means without qualities or attributes, that is, beyond form.) Kabir's Raam is 'nirgun', that is, a divinity without visible qualities or features. It is ever-present, fathomless and beyond mental conception. And yet, it is an intimate and living reality.

Why then does he use the word 'Raam'? There could be several possible reasons. One powerful reason could be that this is the most popular and well-known name of a deity close to the hearts of a large number of people. Thus, it becomes a kind of shorthand to invoke the idea of divinity. A second reason could be for the very sound of the word (see below).

Or it could be for a combination of these two reasons, in the sense that 'Raam' had become a common initiation mantra for many seekers on the spiritual path. Legend has it that Kabir himself, when he used deception to get Ramanand to bless him as his disciple, was given the mantra 'Raam'.

Another thing to note is that Kabir uses the word 'Hari', a name for Krishna, almost as often as Raam. For him, Raam and Hari or other Vaishnavite names such as Govind or Keshav are interchangeable. It can hardly be disputed that when Kabir invokes the name of Raam or Hari, he is speaking of divinity in the abstract, not of particular figures. And yet, it is interesting that he uses particular names to invoke this abstract divinity—a kind of a meeting point of 'sagun' and 'nirgun', making an abstract idea accessible in common parlance. The formless can be invoked through a sound very much 'in form'.

> Raam bhajan bhajyo nahin, nahin kiyo Hari su het
> Ab pachhtaaya kya phire, jab chidiya chug gayi khet?

> You didn't meditate on Raam
> You didn't stay close to Hari
> What's the point of regret now
> When the bird has eaten away your crop?

~

> Bhajo re bhaiya
> Raam, Govind, Hari

Meditate, oh friend
On Raam, Govind, Hari.

In other places, Kabir goes further and makes it starkly clear that the names are not confined to the Vaishnavite tradition. He says bluntly that Rahim (from the Muslim tradition, one of the names of Allah) and Raam denote the same truth. There can be no doubt that he speaks of a higher essence and is not concerned about particular religious or sectarian identities. He himself repudiates such identities.

Hamaare Raam Rahim Karim Kesav
Allah Raam sat soi

My Raam and Rahim, Karim and Krishna
Allah and Raam are the same truth.

And yet, Raam is the word, or shall we say, the sound, most often used by Kabir. Is there something in the sound itself, in the combination of syllables, which carries some power? (Notice the proximity of 'Raam' in sound to 'Rahim' and 'Rehman', the first two names of Allah.) Kabir seems to hint at this himself.

Kabir padhna door kar, pustak dei bahaaye
Baavan aakhar chhod kar, rarai mamai chit laaye

Kabir, stay away from erudition
Throw all the books away!
Forget the letters of the alphabet
Focus your mind on 'Ra' and 'ma'.

❧

Raag Raam ko roop hai, aur Raam raag ke maanhi
Sambhaar ke suna karo, aur dikhne mein kachhu naahin

Melody is the form of Raam
The melody contains Raam
Listen with great attention
It's not visible with the eyes.

So, the essence of Raam is the sound. And sound is important because it is a means to meditation. 'Raam' is important because it is a 'Name', that is, a mantra or a chant, which can be used to focus the mind. This is why the constant exhortation in many songs to 'take the name' or 'remember the name'. The guru, when he or she initiates a disciple, gives him or her a 'name', that is, a particular chant with which to practice. This 'name' is usually a sacred word or set of syllables, or the name of a deity, like 'Om' or 'Raam'.

But Raam is not only the sound. Raam also represents an inner reality, a deeper truth, a subtle fabric. It is something to be found within, not without.

Thaaro Raam hirday mein
Baahar kyon bhatke?

Your Raam is in your heart
Why search outside?

～

Sab van to tulsi bhaye aur parvat Shaligram
Sab nadiyaan Ganga bhayin, jab jaana aatam Raam

All forests became sacred
And all mountains holy
All rivers became like the Ganga
When I found the Raam within.

It is a fine reality, underneath the gross differences of life, which pervades the entire universe, both within and without ('baahar bheetar shabad nirantar' / 'inside outside unbroken sound'). It is contained even in the smallest particle of space. This fine reality is the essence of the world, and of the human being.

Kabir bahut bhatkiya, mann le vishay viraam
Chaalat chaalat jug bhaya, aur til ke ote Raam

Long have you wandered, Kabir
Let the mind cease its quests
You've been searching for ages
In every particle, Raam rests.

It is clear that it is not the outer Raam, over whom people fight, and have been fighting for centuries, who is being invoked. Kabir is bluntly frank in this respect (as in many others). Raam is not an entity over which to fight and dispute. Kabir points to the sheer absurdity of this.

Hindu kahat hai Raam hamaara, Musalmaan Rehmana
Aapas mein dou lade marat hain, marm koi nahin jaana

Hindus claim Raam is theirs
Muslim lay claim to Rehman
They fight and kill each other
Neither knows the essence.

What then is the essence of Raam? Kabir often uses the term 'Raam Ras', or the 'nectar' or 'drink' or 'juice' of Raam, to describe this essence. If Raam is the divinity that pervades all of time and space, tasting its inner essence, its 'rasa', brings great joy and fulfilment.

> Raam ras meetho ghano, jogiya
> Piye amar hoi jaaye
>
> The drink of Raam is extremely sweet, O yogi!
> Whoever drinks it never dies.

Finally, Kabir arrives at a station in himself where he does not even need to take the name of Raam any more. He can claim with supreme confidence that Raam takes *his* name instead, and that Hari follows *him* around, now that his mind has become pure.

> Maala japun na kar japun, aur mukh se kahun na Raam
> Raam hamaara hamein jape, ham paayo bisraam
>
> I don't turn the rosary beads
> I don't chant the name of Raam
> Now Raam chants my name
> And I am at ease!

3

Finding the Guru

~

KABIR grew up in a Muslim household of weavers. Growing up he learnt the trade that he was to practise later, that of weaving. It is an important element in his poetry. Another important element is the spiritual terminology that he employs. Kabir displays limited knowledge of or interest in Islamic theology or even Sufi doctrines, but his deployment and knowledge of the vocabulary of Hatha Yoga is extensive. This has led to some speculation that his family might have been Nathpanthis who had recently converted to Islam. It is also always possible that Kabir himself spent some time with and picked up the vocabulary of the Nathpanthi yogis. One of his earliest biographers, Ananta Das, claims that he spent time in his youth with the Shaktas, adherents of the Tantric tradition. In terms of having a teacher, Kabir's status is not clear. In fact, nothing seems to be very clear about this man, except his own striking, direct expression! Was he self-taught and self-made as a seeker, or did he have a traditional spiritual guru? A legend clarifies and obfuscates at the same time.

The Legend of the Guru

As a young boy or youth, already interested in the spiritual path, Kabir looked around for a teacher or a guru who could train him. Legend says that his choice fixed upon Ramanand, a saintly Brahmanical figure with a large following. Now Kabir knew that Ramanand, being an upper-caste Hindu, would likely refuse to accept him, a low-caste Muslim, as his disciple. So he devised a stratagem.

He was aware that each morning, before dawn, Ramanand climbed down the steps of the ghats to the Ganga for his ritual ablutions. So one morning Kabir went and lay down on one of the steps leading down to the river. In the darkness, Ramanand failed to see the prostrate figure and accidentally stepped on Kabir's forehead.

Spontaneously the following words sprang out of his mouth: 'Raam! Raam!'

Having received the touch of the saint's foot on his forehead, and the mantra of 'Raam' from his tongue, Kabir considered that his deeksha, his initiation, was now complete. He was now Ramanand's disciple and Ramanand was his guru, whether Ramanand himself was aware of it or not.

He subsequently sang songs announcing Ramanand as his guru. When some of Ramanand's disciples complained to him that a lowly Muslim weaver boy by the name of Kabir was going around calling Ramanand his guru, Ramanand asked to see the boy. Legend says that when the guru and disciple were brought face to face, a wordless exchange put a definite seal on their relationship. Kabir went back without a word being uttered on either side.

This legend strongly reinforces the in-between, shifting, ambiguous ground that the figure of Kabir manages to create for himself in the popular imagination. Just as with his birth—neither Hindu nor Muslim, or both—here, too, it is not entirely clear whether

Ramanand was really Kabir's guru or not. Perhaps he was *and* wasn't. The truth, again, proving to be not susceptible to easy dichotomies.

What is remarkable in this story is the fact that even though Kabir ends up with a guru, it is one he has picked out for himself, as well as having picked the time and manner of his initiation. Conventionally, the guru comes upon the disciple and chooses him or her, and decides the time and place of initiation. Kabir overturns the equation, again demonstrating his typical liberating ambiguity—initiated by another *as well as* self-initiated; having an external person as a guru *as well as* really having his guru within (since he hardly spends any time with Ramanand or receives any instruction from him). And so Kabir can boldly claim, as he often does, that the true guru lies within, or as he sometimes says, the guru is in the Word, or is the Word, or is in the sky. Yet, at the same time, he can pay a moving tribute to a real, living guru, as he does to Ramanand in some of his songs. All this despite the fact that, historically speaking, Kabir and Ramanand may not even have been contemporaneous.

Which brings us to the core idea of guru—a key concept not only for Kabir, but for the entire Indic tradition.

Root-Idea: Guru

Guru Govind donon khade, ka ke laagun paaye?
Balihaari Gurudev ki, jine Govind diyo bataaye

Both Guru and Govind stand before me
Whose feet should I touch first?
I surrender to the Guru
Who showed me the path to Govind.

This iconic, much-quoted couplet attributed to Kabir illustrates the central importance of the guru to the Bhakti traditions, and to Indian social fabric in general. The traditional system of learning was located in the 'gurukul' (the guru's abode or literally lineage) in the shape of the 'guru–shishya parampara' (teacher-to-disciple tradition). All transfer of knowledge, whether artistic, philosophic, vocational or spiritual, was embodied and direct, a communication as well as communion between two individuals.

It is against this backdrop that we must look at the central place of the guru in the nirgun Bhakti traditions in general, and in Kabir in particular. The nirgun tradition constantly evokes the formless through the form of words and songs. This delectable dichotomy plays out in the case of the guru as well. The guru is a person, and the guru is not a person. The guru is both outside and within. In song after song, poets acknowledge their flesh-and-blood guru in fulsome terms (Kabir sometimes invokes Ramanand, Gorakhnath is always calling upon Machhinder, some of Meera's songs mention Ravidas, Dharamdas pays tribute to Kabir, and so on). And yet, in an equal number of songs, the guru is described as an essential wisdom, as breath or a current of sound within. The guru is seen as residing within the body, often evoked by the metaphor of the fragile earthen pot, called 'ghat'.

Ya ghat bheetar anhad baaje
Ya hi mein uthat phuwaara

Kahe Kabir suno bhai saadho
Ya hi mein guru hai hamaara
Dhoondhe re dhoondhe andhiyaara

In this body, the sound of the universe
And fountains of elation, in this body

Kabir says, listen seekers
My guru, too, is in this body
Yet you search in the dark!

The guru is like a pool of clear, refreshing water within, and yet we go thirsty. Or the guru is the loaded dice destined to turn the game in our favour, if only we would play.

Guru gam hod bharya ghat bheetar
Moorakh pyaasa jaata bhi kya?

Guru gam paasa haath liya hai
Jeeti baazi haaro bhi kya?

The pool of guru's wisdom overflows within
Why go thirsty, O fool?

The dice of guru's wisdom is in your hands
Why lose a winning hand?

The phrase 'guru gam'—the guru's path, or guru's wisdom—
appears regularly in nirgun Bhakti poetry. It is a stone to keep the
deer from grazing the field or it is a silver band to bind the bristles
of the broom, which sweeps our insides clean. The idea of the guru's
path as the guru itself suits the abstract nirguni sensibility.

How is the guru both a person and not a person, something within
us and someone outside, something inalienable to us and someone to
look up to and revere? This mystery was revealed to me on one of our
many car-rides undertaken in Malwa, Rajasthan or Kutch, interacting
with folk singers. Someone explained very beautifully (I forget
now who it was) that guru is a 'tatva' (a core substance or elemental
essence). That tatva may be incarnate in another person—and then
you bow down to that person as your guru. That tatva also resides in
you, in the moments that you can access it. And then the guru is within.

The guru is many things and can be described in many ways. The
guru is the truth. The guru tatva shows up in all life situations which
teach us something. Or as Prahlad Tipanya, the well-known Malwi
folk singer says, the guru is breath. On the string of the breath we can
chart out a path within. Or in another place he says that the guru is
'samajh', an understanding, guiding us to the truth. Parvathy Baul, a
well-known Baul singer, says that the songs that we sing are the guru.
She once told me personally that the tambura is your guru.

But even more, the guru is 'Shabd', the Word, the primordial
sound within and without. That sound has created the universe. The
ultimate creator is also the ultimate guru.

Guru hamaara gagan mein, chela hai chit maanhi
Surat shabad mela bhaya, kabahu bichhadat naahin

My guru's in the sky
The disciple is in awareness
Attention and Sound thus meet
Never to separate again.

The guru is a potter (kumhaar), a hunter (shikaari), a warrior (soorma), a trader (baniya), a secret agent (bhediya) or a dyer (rangrez). S/he is one who makes the invisible visible, who gives us the roots of wisdom. Guru is the bird up high who sits and watches, while the bird on the lower branch eats the fruit, and enjoys and suffers life (referring to the Upanishadic parable of two birds on a tree). A few illustrations from the Kabir oral traditions.

Guru kumhaar shishya kumbh hai, gadh gadh kaadhe khot
Antar haath sahaar de, aur baahar maare chot

The guru is the potter, disciple the pot
He shapes the pot and irons out flaws
The hand inside gives support
The hand outside beats into shape.

~

Mhaara satguru baniya bhediya
Meri naadi re pakdi re haan

My true guru became an informer
He has his hand on my pulse!

~

Satguru chadhe shikaar pe, haath mein laal kabaan
Moorakh moorakh bach gaye, koi maara sant sujaan

The guru's out on a hunt
Red bow and arrow in hand
The fools escape unhurt
A real seeker is struck down!

Ek daal do panchhi baitha, ek guru ek chela
Chela vo jo phal-phool khaave, guru nirantar khela

Two birds perch on a branch
The guru and the disciple
The disciple eats of the fruit
The guru plays ceaselessly.

There are endless songs about the guru or dedicated to the glory of
the guru in Kabir.

Jag maanganhara,
guru sam daata koi nahin

The world is a beggar
There is no giver like the guru.

Everything is to be offered up to the guru, nothing held back.

Tan mann dhan guruji re arpan
Sees ro naarel chadhaasaan helo

Body, mind, wealth, all for the guru
My head itself an offering.

Such exaltation of the guru can easily slide into a culture of sycophancy towards the human guru. Kabir himself warns against the culture of guru obsession, which contributes to the proliferation of false gurus.

Ye sab guru hain had ke, behad ke guru naahin
Behad aapo upje, anubhav ke ghar maanhi

All these are gurus of limitations
Not gurus of the unbound
In the house of experience
The unbounded arises spontaneously.

Perhaps that's why Kabir repeatedly exhorts us to seek the 'true guru', the satguru. In the age of gurus without number, this raises the question of who is a true guru and who is not. Can one set up shop and 'become' a guru? Kabir frequently uses the term 'satguru' to emphasize this important distinction between a human guru and something that is higher than human. He also resists the pinning down or flattening of the idea of guru—the guru is beyond yes and no, beyond sunlight and shade, beyond any duality.

The terms 'nugura' and 'sugura' are frequent references flowing in the oral traditions of Kabir songs. 'Nugura' is one without a guru, and 'sugura' is one with a guru, a person who is on the path. The 'sugura' makes a good bargain in the bazaar of life, while the 'nugura' loses his capital and wanders around frustrated.

Yo Raam ras mole na beeke, bah rahyo baaraho maaso
Sugura hoye so bhar bhar peeve, nugura jaave re pyaaso

Laagi bajariya tu sauda re kar le, paav rati chaahe maaso
Saudaagir ne sauda re kar liya, moorakh phire udaaso

The nectar of Raam can't be priced or sold
It flows freely through the year
One with a guru drinks her fill
One without, goes thirsty

The market is set up to trade
Transact any amount you like
The trader struck a good bargain
The fool wears a long face.

The guru comes with many names. Kabir singers in the oral traditions constantly play with these names and sing the one they like at any given moment: 'satguru' (true guru), 'dhanguru' (blessed guru), 'dilguru' (guru of the heart), or 'poora guru' (the complete guru). But, in the end, as Kabir says, the guru is a phenomenon that can't be described.

Dharni to kaagaz karun, lekhan karun ban raaye
Saat samandar masi karun, guru gun likha na jaaye

If the whole earth became paper
And all trees became pens
And all the seas became ink
The guru would still be indescribable.

4

Life in the World

~

WHILE Kabir opposed organized religion, ritualism, orthodoxy, hierarchy, and religious hypocrisy all his life, it was not long after his death that various sects came up in his name and organized themselves institutionally (sometimes in the mirror image of what Kabir had been opposing, replicating orthodox ritualism and hierarchies). Followers of some of these sects formed in the name of Kabir ('Kabirpanthis'—those who follow the path of Kabir) do not always warm to the idea that Kabir might have been a man of the world, married and with children. Kabir was a saint—how can he be described as a mere man! (He's invariably referred to as 'Sahib Kabir'—Kabir, the Master.)

This is the same kind of instinct that denies Kabir even a human birth. Instead, in the narrative of some of the sects, he either descended directly from the sky or entered the world through immaculate conception as mentioned earlier.

There is a particular psychology, an unerring instinct, that seeks to separate the men from the saints. If 'saints' are inherently different—

33

not susceptible to birth from a human womb, nor producers of progeny themselves—then this is a kind of excuse for 'ordinary people' to revere and 'follow' saints, on the one hand, and refuse to mould their lives according to the saints' actual exhortations, on the other. Saints are special. Mere mortals are different. Hence, Kabir may be worshipped as an idol but we cannot admit that he's an ordinary man with a wife and kids. This is how some 'gatekeepers' to Kabir's legacy would like to project things. How much more ironic could this be! Like gilded priests claiming to represent Jesus' legacy.

However, there are enough legends and anecdotes to confirm that the masses are happy to accept a Kabir who was very much in the world, a man with a wife and at least two children. Kabir's wife was a woman called Loi, and his children were called Kamaal and Kamaali. Those who want to deny marriage and children to Kabir term Kamaal and Kamaali his disciples.

There is an interesting exchange between Kabir and Kamaal across time and poetry, which is quoted often in popular culture. (There are also songs in the oral traditions attributed to Kamaali, Kabir's daughter and/or disciple.)

Kabir says, in one of his most-quoted dohas:

> Chalti chaaki dekh kar, diya Kabira roye
> In do paatan ke beech mein, saabut bacha na koi

> Seeing the millstones grind
> Kabir laments
> Crushed between the two slabs
> No one is spared.

Kamaal is reputed to have responded to this doha of Kabir with a doha of his own:

Chaaki chaaki sab kahein, kheeli kahe na koi
Jo kheeli se lag raha, va ko baal na baanka hoye

Everyone talks of millstones
No one mentions the pivot
One who reaches the centre
Can't be crushed or destroyed.

The piece of grain that manages to reach the central pivot of emptiness, around which the mill turns and grinds, escapes being destroyed between the crushing stones of duality. While Kabir talks about the inevitability of death, Kamaal brings up the possibility of escape from the cycle of birth and death.

A working man, a family man, Kabir is very much a man of the world. And it is as such that he speaks the people's language, and speaks directly to people, without resorting to theoretical argumentation or scriptural authority. He uses homely, everyday metaphors to make his point, things that everyone can easily relate to. We have already seen the example of the cloth—how, being a weaver himself, he speaks about the body-self as a finely woven cloth. In other places, he uses the metaphor of a clay pot to speak about the human body—how it is brittle, fragile and bound to break one day, just like the pot, dust returning to dust again.

Yeh tan kaacha kumbh hai, liye phire the saath
Thapka laaga phooti gaya, kachhu nahin aaya haath

This body's like a brittle clay pot
We carry it around everywhere
One blow and it shatters!
Nothing to hold on to any more.

In one song he describes the body as a tambura, a folk musical instrument. The breath or mind or self is the string. Tighten it too much and the string snaps! String it too loose and there's no music! It has to be strung just right for it to produce music.

> Yeh tan thaat tambure ka
> Paanch tatva ka bana hai tambura
> Taar laga nau toore ka

> This body, a tambura
> Made of the five elements
> Strung on the nine harmonies.

In other songs he uses the metaphors of gardening or farming or milking the cow, urging his listeners to cultivate well, to prepare the field, to act in time. All these activities of the world root us in everyday reality, pointing to the fact that liberation lies in and through the world, not in escaping from it. This is why it is absurd that some Kabir 'followers' have such an objection to the idea of him being a husband and a father.

Kabir himself very much prefers to describe himself as being in the 'middle of the marketplace' (as opposed to a mountaintop or a forest). He says that real renunciation is of the mind, not of things.

> Jaagan hi mein sovna, sovan hi mein raag
> Ek to ban mein ghar kare, doojo ghar mein rahe beraag

> Sleep within waking
> Attachment within sleep
> One makes a home in the forest
> Another stays at home and is detached.

In another place, he uses the figure of the garden to make the same point. True seekers are those who don't retreat or run away to the forest of renunciation, rather they live in the garden of delights that is this world. But while staying in the garden, they don't consume or ravage it.

> Saadhu aisa chaahiye, dukhe dukhaave naahin
> Paan phool chhede nahin, par rahe baag ke maanhi

> I'm looking for such a seeker
> Who doesn't cause hurt
> Doesn't damage leaves or flowers
> Yet stays in the garden.

Kabir repeatedly uses metaphors related to the bazaar and to business to indicate that transaction is very much of the nature of this world— and the point is not to run away somewhere, but to be the right kind of trader, doing the right kind of transaction.

> Heera pada baazaar mein, khalak ulaanghya jaaye
> Jab aavega paarkhi, sahaje lega uthaaye

> A diamond lies in the market street
> People step over it heedlessly
> When a true jeweller passes by
> He will pick it up immediately.

The metaphor of the market, with the attendant images of striking a good deal or bargain, the jewel that is up for trade, the capital that we have and fritter away, strikes a deep chord, especially in this age of globalized and 'free' markets.

Kabir often describes the sensory world in terms of 'five' and 'twenty-five'. The 'five' often refer quite straightforwardly to the five senses. The five could also refer to the five 'tatvas' or elements of earth, water, fire, air and space. This is often combined with 'teen gun', or the three qualities or forces, which permeate everything in the created universe, known as satva, rajas and tamas in classical Indian philosophy. The five elements and the three forces together represent all of manifest creation (each phenomenon being some combination of these fundamental building blocks). The figure 'five' by itself could also refer to the five 'kleshas' referred to in the yoga traditions, or the five 'evils' usually described as 'kaam, krodh, lobh, moh, ahankaar' (lust, anger, greed, delusion, pride).

The figure of 'twenty-five' most likely comes from Sankhya philosophy, one of the six primary schools of thought in ancient India. Sankhya posits twenty-five basic elements in the universe (the very term 'sankhya' means numbers or arithmetic). The Yoga-sutras of Patanjali accept this division, which then enters Tantric and Hatha Yogic vocabulary. Since Kabir and other saint poets draw heavily upon this vocabulary, it is natural that the figure of twenty-five enters the poetry. The entire enterprise, in simple words, is for consciousness to be able to transcend material creation and experience itself in its pure form. The 'five' and 'twenty-five' stand for the entire sensory experience of the world—all that lies 'out there' and all our inner experience of it.

This brings us to what is one of the most important questions for Kabir: Where is our attention? What are we giving our attention to? This capacity for attention is the capital we have come into the world with. Kabir says that the 'five and twenty-five' are constantly absorbing and, indeed, stealing our attention. All the thoughts and feelings that swirl around within us, provoked by our experiences in the outer world, and which together consume so much of our time and energy.

To return to the metaphor of markets, capital, trade and gems: What is the true jewel, for which there are no takers in this world? In one doha, Kabir laments that we are constantly making the wrong trade, blowing our opportunity.

> Kabir gudadi beekhari, sauda gaya bikaaye
> Khota baandha gaanthadi, khara liya nahin jaaye

> Kabir, the wares were spread
> And the deal was done
> You took the fake gems with glee
> Couldn't pick out the real ones.

Weaving, farming, gardening, cooking, pottery, trading and transacting—this is the stuff of life. Kabir refers to all of this in his repeated invocation of being free *in* the world. This freedom depends on the quality of attention, of awareness, not on running away or renunciation. And this freedom can easily include having a house and a household. Kabir is of the soil, and keeps returning to the soil, even as he can talk in the most abstract terms about attention and awareness.

There is a very interesting legend about how Kabir met his wife, Loi, the mother of his children.

The Legend of Loi

Loi was an orphan girl adopted and raised by a sadhu. When he is about to die, the sadhu prophesies to a grown-up Loi that she would meet her future husband shortly and the sign to recognize him is that he would respond to all her questions with the same answer.

Loi is puzzled by this. How could anyone respond to different questions with the same answer? But she doesn't doubt her adoptive father's word and stores this information in her memory.

The sadhu passes away. Sometime later, a party of a man accompanied by five sadhus arrives at her hut, and requests refreshments. Loi brings milk for all of them. The man divides the milk into six equal parts and distributes five cups to the five waiting sadhus. As he is about to drink the milk from the sixth cup himself, he abruptly stops and puts down his cup. Loi asks him why he's not having the milk. The man replies that he's sensed that there is another sadhu coming shortly and that he's keeping the milk for him.

Sure enough, after a few moments, another sadhu turns up at Loi's hut. The man hands him the last, untouched cup of milk without a word.

Loi gets very intrigued by this man. How did he know that another sadhu would be arriving soon when he did not expect him just a few moments earlier? She feels like getting to know more about the man. She begins to ask him questions.

'What is your name?' she asks.

'Kabir,' he responds.

'What is your caste?' she asks.

'Kabir,' he responds.

'What is your religion?' she asks.

'Kabir,' he responds.

'What is the name of your sect?' she asks.

'Kabir,' he responds.

'Which group do you belong to?' she demands at last, trying different tacks, desperate to pin him down.

'Kabir,' he responds, unfazed.

That's when Loi realizes that this is the man her father had prophesied about. The man with the same answer to all questions!

There is a Kabir doha addressing this ordinary human need to pigeonhole people into fixed identities, which Kabir resists at every turn.

Jaat hamaari aatma, praan hamaara naam
Alakh hamaara isht hai, aur gagan hamaara gaam

Soul, my caste
Breath, my name
The invisible, my deity
The sky, my hometown.

In another famous doha, he comments on this widespread obsession with outer markers of identity.

Jaat na poochho saadhu ki, poochh leejiye gyaan
Mol karo talwaar ka, padi rehne do myaan

Don't ask about a seeker's caste
Ask about his wisdom
Value the sword within
Not the outer sheath.

This legend brings us to another core idea in Kabir, and a fundamental question of human existence itself—that of identity. Who *are* we? Who am 'I'? Where have I come from? Where am I going? And how do our notions of identity relate to separations and divisions in the world, that is, the sphere of 'duality'?

Root-Idea: Main–Tu | Identity/Duality

Main-meri jab jaayegi, tab aavegi aur
Jab mann nishchal bhaya, tab paavega thor

If all this 'me' and 'mine' ended
Then there would be space
When the mind becomes still
It finds its resting-place.

The 'I' takes up a lot of space. Small word, huge demands! This seeming non-entity is at the centre of everything. Our individual universes revolve around this tiny 'I'.

Yet, in the thought of Kabir, this all-consuming 'I' is preventing the vast divine from showing itself to us.

Jab main tha tab Hari nahin, ab Hari hai main naahin
Prem gali ati saankri, ya mein dou samaaye naahin

When I was, Hari wasn't
Now Hari is, I am not
The path of love is extremely narrow
Two cannot fit in it.

In another doha, Kabir seems to suggest that the dissolution of the self, the erasure of this tyrannical 'I', and the erasure of the duality between the individual and the divine, leads to a dissolving of the sense of separation that plagues all other earthly relationships—between the self and the spouse, relative, neighbour, friend, enemy, or stranger.

Main laga us ek se, ek bhaya sab maanhi
Sab mera main saban ka, tahaan doosra naahin

I merged with that one
Became one with everything
All are mine, I belong to all
There is no other.

The 'I' gets replaced by 'you', which merges into the all-encompassing
'You' that permeates the universe.

Tu-tu karta tujh gaya, mujh mein rahi na hun
Vaara pheri bali gayi, jit dekhun tit tu

Chanting your name, I passed into you
No 'me' remained in my 'I'
The cycle of becoming was sacrificed
Now wherever I look, I see you.

This is a bewildering universe that Kabir seems to be speaking
about, which makes little or no sense to our small minds caught up
in the notion of establishing our separate identities. For us it's very
important to establish our self-image, self-esteem, self-respect or self-
worth, in a social sense, in distinction to 'others'. In Kabir's universe,
on the other hand, there is a vast merging happening. Words, concepts
and images become meaningless.

Kehna tha so keh diya, ab kuchh kaha na jaaye
Ek raha dooja gaya, dariya leher samaaye

I said all I had to
Now nothing more to say

One stayed, no other remained
Like a wave merges in the ocean.

These dohas seem to put in a nutshell Kabir's essential feeling about duality and unity, otherness and oneness. If the ego may be defined as the sense of separation (and therefore individuality and uniqueness), these words seem to describe a state beyond the ego, where the sense of separation (and therefore the pain of incompleteness) is transcended. This is a place of joy and exhilaration.

Kabir hints at this much larger perspective in the famous song, 'Yugan yugan ham yogi'. He describes himself, in this larger sense, as a seeker through several ages, for time out of mind, a veritable eternity. Here a much more comprehensive sense of the 'I' comes through.

Sabhi thor jamaat hamri, sabhi thor par mela
Ham sab maan, sab ham maan, ham hain bahuri akela

In every place a gathering, my gathering
In every place, a carnival
I am in all, all are in me
I am many and alone.

The usual 'I', with which we live, also posits an 'other'. Hell is other people, as Jean-Paul Sartre famously said. When one is deeply invested in a small idea of the self, one can tend to construct a demonic, threatening other—whether on the basis of race, gender, caste, class, nationality, or any other category. Difference gets magnified. All faults and darkness seem to lie with this demonic other, in opposition to whom we define ourselves. But as Kabir says:

Avval Allah noor upaaya, kudrat ke sab bande
Ek noor se jag upaajya, ko bhale ko mande?

First and foremost, Allah's radiance
All humans come from God
The same light created the whole world
Who is 'good' and who is 'bad'?

Hindu mue hain Raam kahi, Musalmaan Khudaai
Kahe Kabir so jeevta, dui mein kadai na jaai

Hindus die muttering Raam
Muslims die chanting Khuda
Kabir says that one really lives
Who never enters into duality.

In other words, to divide is to be dead. To be whole is to be really living! Both the demonic and the divine seem to reside within oneself. Perhaps there is no 'other'. As Eckhart Tolle puts it in *Stillness Speaks*: 'Ultimately, of course, there is no other, and you are always meeting yourself.'

Is this what is meant when Kabir says that the path of love is extremely narrow? In this sense, perhaps, love is like death—one of two has to die. Duality, or separation, is a big burden, and the path is delicate. As Kabir says in his famous song, 'Ishq mastana':

Kabira ishq ka maata, dui ko door kar dil se
Jo chalna raah naazuk hai, haman sir bojh bhaari kya?

Kabir, get drunk on love
And rid your heart of duality!
Such a delicate path to tread
Why lug a heavy load on your head?

The Upanishads speak of the perilousness of the spiritual path using
the figure of a razor's edge. The level of concentration, alertness,
one-pointedness, required to negotiate it is immense. Lightness is
essential; othering people creates heaviness and distortion of vision.

Sharp like a razor's edge is the path,
The sages say, difficult to traverse.
    (The *Katha Upanishad*, translation by Eknath Easwaran)

Otherness is often represented in the world by different colours—
the different colours of various national flags, or the different
colours associated with different religions or sects. To lose this may
be what is meant by 'becoming one colour'.

Laali mere laal ki, jit dekhun tit laal
Laali dekhan main gayi, to main bhi ho gayi laal

My beloved's coloured in red
Now wherever I look, I see red
I set out in search of red
I became red myself.

In the song 'Ghat ghat mein panchhi bolta' (This bird sings in each
and every body), Kabir speaks about the one hiding inside the many.

Aap hi dandi, aap taraaju, aap hi baitha tolta
Aap hi maali, aap bageecha, aap hi kaliyaan todta

You're the pivot, you the scales
You are the one who weighs
You're the gardener, you the garden
You the one plucking flowers.

In another song, 'Tu ka tu' (You, only you), he playfully dissolves a series of dualities.

Choron ke sang chori karta, badmaashon mein bhedo tu
Chori kar ke tu tu bhag jaave, pakadne vaala tu ka tu

Nar naari mein ek viraaje, do duniya mein deese kyon?
Baalak ban kar rovan laage, raakhan vaala tu ka tu

Among thieves, you're a thief
Among criminals, you are one
You steal and you run away
The cop who nabs you is also you!

One in both man and woman
Why do we keep seeing two?
As a child, you begin to cry
The one who pacifies you is also you!

It is astonishing how many poets across the ages have spoken of the same idea—that the one resides in the many, that the masks are several but the actor is one. That the forms are different but the essence is the same.

Kabir kuaan ek hai, panihaari anek
Bartan sabke nyaare hain, par paani sab mein ek

Kabir says, the well is one
Water-bearers many
Each one has a different vessel
But they all contain the same water

(Poet: Kabir)

≈

Khud kooza-o, khud koozaagar-o, khud gil-e-kooza
Khud rind-e-subu kash
Khud bar sar-e-aan kooza khareedaar baraamad
Bishkast-o ravaan shud

He is the potter, the clay and the cup
He, the one who drinks from the cup
He is the one who buys the drink
And he the one who breaks the cup and leaves

(Poet: Rumi)

≈

Aap hi bhaati, aap hi madghar, aap hi hot kalaala
Aap hi peeve, aap pilaave, aap phire matwaala

You're the brewery, you the bar, you're the bartender
You're the one drinking and supplying, you the drunk gone
under!

(Poet: Sachal Sarmast)

Fariduddin Ayaz, a renowned Sufi qawwal based in Karachi, Pakistan,
speaks about the purpose of duality as well as its essential emptiness:

'To understand anything, to comprehend reality, we split it into two. Like there is you and me. When we try to see ourselves, we use a mirror. You comprehend yourself through the illusion created by the mirror. But there is nothing in the mirror.'

If one breaks through the overpowering illusion, perhaps one can see the one reality. This is the powerful, well-known mystic idea of rending the veil. That is why Kabir says: 'Ghoonghat ke pat khol, tohe piya milenge' (Lift up the veil and you will see the beloved).

5

Trust in the Sacred

A feature of how Kabir is appropriated by different groups is his being marshalled for strikingly different purposes. Social activists tend to view Kabir as a radical revolutionary, striking at the very heart of caste and religious prejudices, speaking truth to power fearlessly. This is a romantic and alluring view of Kabir, with a large amount of truth in it. But this truth is partial.

Kabir's 'followers' on the other hand—Kabir didn't want any followers, he only asked for fellow seekers to walk with him—tend to elevate him to the status of saint or even God, someone not at all of this world. For them Kabir came from and is speaking about realms ('lokas') much beyond the human dimension.

Other, earlier commentators tried to paint Kabir as a Vaishnavite devotee in the orthodox lineage of Ramanand. In this view, Kabir is a proponent of traditional Vaishnava bhakti (invoked in the figures of Raam and Krishna).

None of these conceptions—always partial, always incomplete— do justice to the full power and extent of the figure of Kabir. He is *at once* a social revolutionary and a most sincere devotee. He is at the same time intellectually rigorous, supremely critical of social hierarchies *and* deeply reverential of the divine, which he calls by many names, not just the Vaishnava ones. Again, 'both/and', not 'either–or'.

A sense of the sacred pervades Kabir's poetry. There is no getting away from it. To miss or overlook this element, as many left-leaning social activists do, is to miss half the point of Kabir's poetry. On the other hand, to overlook or gloss over his critiques of hypocrisy, power structures and hierarchy obscures his razor-sharp gaze.

Kabir is nothing if not critical. And yet he makes his scathing social critiques *on the basis of* his absolute trust in the sacred, in a higher dimension, something beyond the merely human. Kabir is not a 'humanistic' poet in this sense at all. His solutions are not the solutions of Marx or of postmodern 'social scientists'. Kabir is a poet of the sacred. There is meaning in the world and in human life. And the meaning of being human lies in the beyond-human.

> Tum kas baaman, ham kas sooda, ham kas lahu ho, tum kas doodha?
> Tu kas baaman bamani jaaya, to aan dwaar se kaahe nahin aaya?

> Ek haad, maas, mal, moota, ek rudir ek gooda
> Ek boond se srishti rachyo hai, ko baaman ko sooda?

> How are you a Brahmin, I a Shudra?
> I have blood in my veins, and do you have milk?
> If you're born of a high, noble woman
> Why didn't you enter the world from another gate?

> The same bones, flesh, shit, piss
> The same heart and liver

The same drop created the whole universe
Who is a Brahmin, who a Shudra?

This drop of oneness that has created the whole universe is the ground on which Kabir stands, claiming to have known it himself, within himself, by experience. It is something more real than what appears to be caste or social reality. That is why he can critique them fearlessly. This other reality is the fabric of existence itself, which he has seen. This is what gives him the strength to speak truth to power.

Jaati julaaha kya kare, hirday base Gopal
Kabir Raamaiya kanth milu, chookahi sab janjaal

What's all this talk of 'low caste'
Gopal lives within my heart
Kabir has embraced his Raam
He's out of all this mess.

So powerful is this connection with the One that Kabir is able to invest all trust and reliance in that connection. There are a couple of legends from Kabir's life which evoke this sense of trust in the sacred in an ironic and comic manner. Let's look at both these legends and reflect on what they might be pointing towards.

The Legend of the Feast

As we shall see in the next chapter, Kabir managed to make a fair amount of enemies in his lifetime. Most prominent among them were the pandits and the mullahs, gatekeepers of organized religion, with their power, prestige and wealth threatened by the force of Kabir's message.

So, once upon a time, one pandit hit upon what seemed to him an excellent idea to make trouble for Kabir. He sent out an invitation in Kabir's name to all the sadhus of Varanasi and surrounding villages to come the next day for a grand feast at Kabir's house.

As word went around rapidly and spread like wildfire, sadhus began to show up at Kabir's door from the next morning onwards, expecting to be treated to a fare fit for the gods. A biggish crowd gathered. The gathering began to murmur and grow restive rapidly as there were no visible signs of preparations for a grand feast.

When Kabir realized what had happened and saw all the hungry sadhus gathered outside his small hut, unreasonably expecting a big party from a poor weaver, he quietly slipped out of the back door. In other words, he ran away. He left the sadhus and his house to their own devices and headed into the jungle to sit quietly and meditate.

Towards evenfall, as he was sitting quietly under a tree, he saw a group of sadhus, looking well fed and thoroughly cheerful, coming towards him. They did not recognize Kabir and thought that he was just another poor sadhu.

One of them said to him eagerly: 'Hey, what are you doing here? Don't sit and waste your time. There is a big feast on at Kabir's house, over there, with unlimited supply of food and the best dishes. Look at us—we've eaten well! Go and partake of it yourself, before it is too late!'

When Kabir heard this, he smiled and was amused. God had obviously taken care of his troubles. When he reached home he found that all who had come had been generously and adequately fed. God's bottomless pot had been overflowing.

And the legend says precisely this. That it was Hari himself who dressed up as Kabir and brought with him enough food to feed all the invitees.

This story obviously echoes an episode from the Mahabharata, where the Pandavas in exile receive a visit from the sage Durvasa and his disciples. Unable to feed them because they had already finished eating themselves, the Pandavas and their wife Draupadi are anxious about the hospitality that is due to the sage. While Durvasa and his disciples go to the river to bathe themselves to prepare for the meal, Draupadi sits down disconsolate and, in her despair, prays to Krishna. Krishna appears and straightaway asks Draupadi for some food, claiming that he's hungry. Draupadi begins to weep. She'd called on Krishna to help her in her hour of trouble and here he is himself asking for food when she has none. She confesses to him that she has nothing to give him. Krishna asks her if she's sure, and tells her to check again. She brings her cooking pot, the famous Akshaypatra ('limitless vessel') of Yudhishthir, and Krishna sees that there is a single grain of rice sticking to the bottom of the pot. He prises it out. This will be quite enough for me, he says, and eats it.

The hunger of the whole universe, says the story, is appeased in that moment. Durvasa and his disciples bathing in the river feel satiated. They have no more desire to eat. Embarrassed that a meal might already have been prepared for them, they slip away quietly. The Pandavas heave a sigh of relief.

The Akshaypatra—the vessel that never runs out—was a boon given to Yudhishthir to be able to feed various visitors during the Pandavas' period of exile in the forest. It would run out only once Draupadi had fed all the visitors and eaten herself. Durvasa, motivated by the Pandavas' arch-enemy Duryodhana, had arrived just after she'd eaten, hence the crisis.

A crisis that is beyond a human solution is resolved by a higher agency/dimension, in the case both of the Pandavas and of Kabir. In the latter instance, Kabir does nothing more than run away from the scene and meditate under a tree. Did God really appear in his stead with the food? Or was the sadhus' hunger appeased magically, as was Durvasa's? Or is it that unexpected things can happen when one remains equanimous even in the face of a terrifying crisis? The understanding of such fables requires an appreciation of the mythic imagination.

There is a legend around the Buddha where he is falsely accused by a seemingly pregnant woman of being the father of the unborn baby. The woman has been put up to this lie by the Buddha's enemies. She ties a soft pillow around her belly under her dress and claims to be pregnant. The people gathered around start to hurl abuses at the Buddha, calling him a corrupt ascetic and a hypocrite, and they bay openly for his blood. The Buddha remains calm in the face of the absurd accusation and the very real threats, and merely smiles. At that moment, the legend says, the thread tying the pillow under the woman's dress gives way, the fabric having been weakened previously by a mouse. The pillow falls and the truth is revealed.

The stories embody an archetypal truth. Once one does not respond to a crisis with fear, and retains faith, trust and confidence, even adverse situations are likely to turn around, sooner or later.

In the words of one of the most famous verses of Kabir, spoken in God's voice:

> Khoji hue turat mil jaaun, ik pal ki talaash mein
> Kahat Kabir suno bhai saadho, main to hoon vishwaas mein
>
> If you look for me, you'll find me
> In a second's search, in an instant
> Kabir says, listen fellow seekers
> I reside in the quality of trust.

This brings us to the next legend, which runs along similar lines.

The Legend of God Begs for Cloth

One day, the day of the weekly bazaar perhaps, Kabir takes the cloth he has woven through the week and goes to the market to sell it. He sits down at his usual spot and awaits buyers, so that he can earn some money, buy some grains for the coming week, and feed his family.

Hari decides to test Kabir's devotion.

Along comes a poor, hobbling, half-naked sadhu, who is Hari himself in disguise. The poor sadhu whines and pleads with Kabir, begging for some cloth, claiming that he has no food to eat, nor any cloth to properly cover himself with. Kabir gives him half the cloth that he has brought to the market to sell.

After a short while, a Muslim fakir turns up at Kabir's spot and asks for some cloth with the same excuses. This is also Hari himself, in another guise. Without hesitation Kabir hands him the remaining half of the cloth that he had intended to sell.

Left with no cloth, and having earned no money to buy food, with hungry stomachs waiting at home, what does Kabir do? He runs away!

He simply walks away from the market and the house, and into the jungle to meditate. In the evening when he returns home he can smell the wonderful aromas of his wife's cooking. Intrigued, he asks her where she got the money from to buy supplies.

Loi explains that a wealthy merchant (Hari in a third disguise) showed up at the door in the afternoon. He claimed to have bought two pieces of wonderfully woven cloth from a sadhu and a fakir. The cloth was so fine that he felt that he had not paid adequately for it, and wanted to reward the weaver of the cloth himself. The sadhu and fakir had pointed him to Kabir's home, he claimed. And he had come to express his gratitude for the finely woven cloth through a generous offering. Kabir and his family feast on a wonderful and satisfying meal.

In both the stories narrated here, as we can see, a meal is supplied, consumed and enjoyed, whether by the sadhus or by Kabir with his family. The symbolic significance of course is one of abundance as opposed to lack. In God's house there is no want, neither spiritual nor material.

There are at least two ways to read this second story. I happen to like both of them. The first is the obvious one. Kabir, unable to help himself in giving his cloth away to the needy, but then bewildered by how he would face his family, had simply run away from the scene and trusted God to take care of things. The second is that Kabir *recognized* Hari in the guise of the sadhu and the fakir. And he knew, with absolute assurance, that if Hari himself had taken the cloth, he would return adequate and fair compensation. So Kabir didn't need to worry and could leave everything in Hari's hands. (And the deeper significance of Hari taking the cloth and paying for it is that *everyone* is Hari, both the givers and the takers. This is the essential lesson of oneness.)

What I enjoy in both these stories is the simple fact that Kabir runs away! It makes him all the more human. Confronted by kings or priests with power, of course, Kabir never backs down, as we shall see. But in these cases he trusts the divine and sidesteps the clutches of the crises. It is also a way of saying, perhaps, that he trusts in the power of the universe, or the sacred, and relies on something greater than just his mind or his ego. And then help comes to him.

There is a very funny song attributed to Kabir in the oral traditions, in which Kabir speaks ironically in the voice of his exasperated wife. Loi is fed up of Kabir's impractical ways and complains in a typical fashion to her mother-in-law about her useless son.

Who Misled My Kabir?

Kabiro mhaaro, kin nar ne bhurmaayo Kabiro mhaaro?

Ann nahin khaave, paani nahin peeve
Naina neend kadi nahin sove
Jaan kahin dekhe sat sangat ko
Vahin daude ni chalyo jaave, Kabiro mhaaro

Ek din ka sau gaj bunta
Soi haat lai jaato
Jo koi dekhe nanga ugaadha
Odhai pehrai ne ghare aato, Kabiro mhaaro

Kehti bahuvad suno saasuji
Aisa poot ke kyon jaayo
Inka mann mein aisi thi to
Mhaare parni ne kyon laayo, Kabiro mhaaro

Kahe Kabir suno bhai saadho
Aage to jhagdo machega
Sab hil mil kar lo nivedo, Kabiro mhaaro

Oh Kabir!
Who put him on the wrong track?

Doesn't eat or drink any more
His eyes get no sleep
Wherever he sees truth-seekers gathered
Goes running there, my Kabir
Who misled him?

Weaves yards of cloth each day
And heads off to the market
But let him see anyone in tatters
Gives the whole cloth away, my Kabir
Who put him on the wrong track?

Mother-in-law, listen to the bride
Why did you beget such a son?
If his mind was turned this way
Why did he marry me, my Kabir?
Who misled him?

Kabir says, listen seekers
Looks like there's trouble brewing
Let's put our heads together
And get out of this mess
Who put him on the wrong track?

Trust in something higher is often seen in conventional parlance as sheer craziness or 'being on the wrong track'. We who are so modern and up-to-date, who trust only our limited minds and reason and logic, often bungle things up spectacularly and leave things worse than how they were before we touched them. The cure is often worse than the disease. Our interventions solve one problem and create ten more. We lack a holistic grasp of things and cover up one leak only to expose two others.

Trust in something higher does not mean not acting. It means being humble, listening, seeing without the ego's agitations (fear or desire), and then acting from a place of holistic knowledge and understanding. It means knowing when to act and when to hold back. It joins the power of truth to one's actions.

Jab lag meri, meri kare, tab lag kaaj ekai na sare
Jab meri, meri mati jaaye, tab Hari kaaj savaare aaye

As long as we chant I, I, I
All our acts are haphazard and awry
When we destroy the obsession with I
Hari himself makes our actions worthwhile.

Root-Idea: Sahaj | Simple, Easy, Spontaneous

Sahaj sahaj sab koi kahe, sahaj na cheenhe koi
Jin sahaje Hari mile, sahaj kaheeje soi

Everyone speaks of 'sahaj', of simplicity
No one understands its meaning
She who attains Hari with simplicity
Call her the 'sahaj' one.

Sahaj is a word immediately understood by native speakers, yet not easy to translate or explain. It is used in several different contexts and ways. In the most common usage, it points to when something is, or has become, *easy*: natural, unforced and without effort. For Kabir, sahaj, like prem (love), is connotative of the highest value.

It is like a skill that one takes hours and hours to master and to perfect, and which, finally, becomes so much a part of oneself that it is no longer any effort at all. The difficult becomes simple, the seemingly impossible becomes natural. Difficulties of being itself, in this state, are resolved into an essential simplicity of being. When one finally sees the truth, one cannot understand how one roamed around in complexities of falsehood for so long. Sahaj is the place where the ultimate sophistication ends in startling simplicity.

In traditional Indian philosophy, sahaj indicates a state of mind and being beyond striving for something—in which there is no gap between the word and the deed, the conception and the execution, the vision and the reality, the object and the self. In other words, it indicates a state of no alienation. In Hatha Yoga, it is one of the synonyms of samadhi, the ultimate state.

W.M. Callewaert says that the word sahaj 'denotes that which is part of oneself, which one does not have to make an effort to obtain ... It may be translated as "absence of conscious or strained endeavour'.[2]

In its etymological sense, 'sahaja' means 'arising together' (saha=with, or together; and ja=being born, arising). This links it to the Buddhist idea of co-dependent origination, that is, the interdependent and simultaneous arising of everything. Nothing has an existence by itself, but only in relation to all other things. Things don't exist as solid, separate, autonomous entities—but in relation to each other.

It is not just that things *were* simultaneously arisen at some point but that they *are* simultaneously arisen each moment, in each alive moment of perception. Like in an electronic image, nothing exists discretely or in isolation—at the bottom of it there are just pixels—only in the act of perception does the image exist as we see it. Alter the perception and we would see a different image.

We tend to think of people as isolated and discrete entities. 'You' are separate from 'I', 'us' from 'them', 'him' from 'her'. But, as Kabir keeps reminding us, things are intimately connected with each other. 'Raam' with 'Rahim', 'I' with 'you'. Perhaps to understand this basic truth is, in a sense, to be 'simplified', to become free of the imaginary complexities of an imaginary self and a divisive social reality.

In this sense, sahaj has also been explained as the simultaneous experience of 'samsara' and 'nirvana' (the bonds of the world and the liberation from them), and therefore a transcending of troubling dualities.[3] All oppositions, artificially set up by the mind—bondage and liberation, earth and heaven, action and meditation, now and hereafter—are dissolved.

Using another term, we may say that sahaj is swabhava, one's intrinsic nature. In this sense, sahaj can be understood as 'spontaneously arising'. As the nature of fire is to burn, the nature of tree to grow and give fruit, the nature of water to flow, so to seek and find its own truth is the nature of consciousness. To realize at last one's own true nature is to become 'sahaja', or natural. This is a place of rest, of bliss, and of transcendence of complexity and difficulty.

The notion of 'sahaj' became central in a certain strand of Indian spirituality through various Buddhist, Tantric and Nathpanthi traditions. From around the eighth century onward, the notion of 'sahaj' and 'sahajavastha' (in the sense of an 'arrived state') became quite important in these traditions. Since then, it has grown and thrived in the poetry of the Bhakti saints, and in the Baul and Vaishnava 'Sahajiya' traditions. Kabir inherited this entire spiritual universe and its vocabulary.

A popular spiritual usage of the term is in the notion of 'sahaj samadhi'. This is when the state of 'samadhi', the highest stage of meditation or awareness, becomes constant or natural. Ramana Maharshi describes it as 'remaining in the primal, pure, natural state without effort'.

While the 'sahaj' state of the Hatha Yogis was a hard-won one, achieved as a result of many austerities and practices, Kabir scholar Hazariprasad Dwivedi argues that Kabir's 'sahaj' is a much more spontaneous state, claimed without having to renounce the world or kith or kin, or having to adopt specific practices.[4] Kabir does seem to oppose elaborate practices ('jap tap') with his emphasis on the 'sahaj'. For him, in this sense, meditation and being in the world are not separate things.

Santon, sahaj samaadhi bhali
Aankh na moondun, kaan na roondhun, kaaya kasht na
dhaarun
Khule nain main hans hans dekhun, sundar roop nihaarun

Kahun so naam, sunun so sumiran, jo kuchh karun so pooja
Grah-udyaan eksam dekhun, bhaav mitaaun dooja

Seekers, spontaneous, ever-present awareness is best.
I don't close my eyes, don't stop my ears,
I don't torture my body.
With open eyes I behold the beauty of form and smile
Whatever I say is mantra, whatever I hear is wisdom,
Whatever I do is prayer.
I view both home and forest with an equal eye,
And destroy the feeling of otherness.

Happiness, fulfilment, the nectar of Raam, are all a function of this state.

Hai kou sant sahaj sukh upje, jaako jap-tap deun dalaali
Ek boond bhari Raam ras, jyon bhari deyi kalaali

Is there a saint of spontaneous bliss
I'll trade him all my spiritual practices
To fulfil with one drop of Raam-nectar
Like the bartender fills a glass of wine.

How is this state of 'sahaj' to be reached? Kabir describes this in a doha.

Jitni leher samoond mein, utni mann ki daud
Sahaje moti neepje, jab mann aave hai thor

The mind has as many turns
As there are waves in the ocean

The pearl forms naturally, spontaneously
When the mind is stilled.

And when this state is reached, meditation does not have to be 'done',
it happens spontaneously; awareness does not have to be 'maintained',
it arises and stays by itself, which is 'sahaj samadhi'.

Rag rag mein bole Raam ji, aur rom rom rarankaar
Sahaje hi dhun upje, so hi sumiran saar

Raam chants in my every vein
And resounds in every pore
The vibration arises spontaneously
This is the essence of meditation.

6

The Firebrand and Iconoclast

~

I T is not for nothing that Kabir has acquired a reputation for being a firebrand. We have seen in one doha how he speaks of standing in the midst of the marketplace with a flaming torch in hand. Only those who can burn their houses down can walk with him. In a fuller song along the same lines, he promises something in return for the burning. Burn your house and a new one will arise to take its place.

Main mera ghar jaadiya re, jogiya ji
Liyo paleeta haath
Koi agar jaado ghar aapro re, jogiya ji
Chalo hamaare saath

Raam ras meetho ghano re, jogiya ji
Piye amar hoi jaaye

Ghar jaadyo ghar ubhre re, jogiya ji
Ghar raakhyo ghar jaaye

Ek achambho main dekhiyo re, jogiya ji
Mado kaal ne khaaye

I burnt down my house, yogi
I took up the flaming torch
If you scorch your own house, yogi
Then join me on this walk.

The drink of Raam is incredibly sweet
One who drinks it never dies.

Scorch the house and a new one arises, yogi
Protect it and it's gone!
I saw a miraculous sight, yogi
A dead man eating up time.

Kabir is fearless in his taking on of caste and religious orthodoxy, and their representatives, the pandit and the mullah. I have heard it said—and only half in jest—that if Kabir were alive today, he would either be in a hospital (beaten up), or in jail (accused of sedition), or in a mental asylum (deemed crazy)![5] As we shall see in the next chapter, Kabir faced his fair share of persecution in his own time.

Right now we focus on Kabir's sensational jousts with the gatekeepers of organized religion, the power-brokers of the time, the sanctified 'experts', that is, the priestly class among both the Hindus and the Muslims. (He treats them both with equal disdain.) The matter is truly sensational because it couldn't have been common then, as it isn't now, to speak the truth so fiercely and loudly and clearly and fearlessly.

Paahan pooje Hari mile, toh main poojun pahaad
Ta se toh chakki bhali, pees khaaye sansaar

If by worshipping a stone you could find God
I would worship a big mountain!
A better use of stone is the grinding mill
It provides flour for the whole world.

Kankar patthar jod ke masjid liyo chunaaye
Ta chadh Mullah baang de, kya behra hua Khudaai?

Scrambling some bricks together
You built a great mosque
The mullah climbs to the roof and shouts
Has God gone deaf?

While the priests insisted that only a few could enter the temples (they were out of bounds for the 'lower castes'), Kabir said quite baldly that God does not reside in the temple. And while the priests claimed that truth could only be found (via them) in the holy books and scriptures, such as the Vedas and the Qur'an, Kabir said equally bluntly that the truth lay within one's own body, that books were not required, and that knowledge is a thing of experience not of the intellect.

No wonder Kabir was not popular with the priests. He was hurting their business! Some of us in our own times might feel that we are beyond such 'medieval superstition' and therefore we can join with Kabir in his wit and mocking laughter. But who are our own priests, whom we follow without question? Economists? Scientific experts? Politicians and the media? Have we really overcome our socially conditioned inability to go against the grain, to not follow the herd, to stand out? Kabir is an iconoclast. Which means that he's a breaker of holy images. What are our own holy cows that we cling to quite passionately and blindly?

The consequences of taking a contrary stand can often be perilous while agreeing with conventional wisdom can be rewarding. Do we have the courage of our convictions, as Kabir did?

> Saadho dekho jag bauraana
> Saach kaho to maaran dhaave
> Jhoothe jag patiyaana

> Seekers, look, the world has gone mad
> If you speak the truth, they beat you up
> If you speak falsehoods, they believe you.

A few legends speak of Kabir's encounters with the so-called holy men, those with a ponderous sense of their own importance.

The Legend of the Dirty Cup

One afternoon, during the heat of the day, a group of sadhus was making their way towards the Ganga. They passed close to Kabir's hut and thought to ask for a drink of water. Kabir was called out and he was only too happy to oblige.

As he brought out a pot of water and some earthen cups, one of the sadhus had a suspicion about the caste of this man. Obliquely at first, and then directly, they enquired about the caste of the man about to serve them water. Kabir replied that he was a weaver. The sadhus refused to drink water from the cups touched by the hands of a weaver, a 'low-caste' man.

Kabir had a hearty laugh at this response. Much to the sadhus' chagrin, far from being ashamed at daring to offer water to them, this man seemed highly amused and couldn't stop laughing. They grew angry and upset.

'What is this impertinence, you insolent fellow!' one of them shouted.

'How dare you laugh at us?' demanded another.

'Can't you see who we are?' said another.

Calming himself down in order to answer them, Kabir said:

'This water which I offered you is from the holy river Ganga. If this water couldn't purify me or my cups, how is it going to cleanse you of your many sins? The illogicality of you "learned men" is what is making me laugh.'

The Legend of Jahangast

Jahangast was a well-known Muslim fakir. But he was ambitious and desired to be even better known than he was presently. He had heard that many people seemed to throng to this poor, low-caste weaver called Kabir. They couldn't stop raving about him. But who was this paltry, two-bit weaver compared to him, Jahangast, who should rightly be celebrated as the greatest living fakir?

In such a fashion some 'fakirs' have a distorted notion of what it means to be a fakir. Shafi Muhammad Faqir, a Sufi singer from Sindh, Pakistan, sings a couplet describing the qualities of a true fakir. The Arabic word is made up of four letters: 'fay', 'kay', 'yay' and 'ray'. Fay, he says, stands for 'fikr', or constant contemplation of the divine. Kay, for 'kifaayat', or austerity. Yay, for 'yaqeen', or trust. And ray, for 'riyaazat', or practice. A true fakir is a combination of all these qualities. To be a real fakir—just like being a real Sufi or a real yogi—is a very high station. But then, as now, anyone with enough ambition could claim to be a fakir or a sufi or a yogi!

So Jahangast, the great 'fakir', decided to defeat Kabir in one way or another, and prove himself the superior one. He would humiliate this low-caste weaver. With great fanfare he announced to the whole world that he was going to visit Kabir in his hut and prove once and for all who was the greatest fakir among them. Kabir, being a householder, did not strictly qualify for the epithet. But Kabir did sing of 'fakiri', and he had acquired many followers, which is what Jahangast was really eyeing.

As Jahangast approached Kabir's hut, followed by a great and curious crowd, Kabir quickly fetched a pig covered in slime and tied it outside his door. As Jahangast drew nearer he was disgusted at the sight of the pig and offended on account of his Muslim faith. He started complaining loudly, saying that this filthy pig showed the truth about Kabir, and refused to enter the compound.

Kabir came out of the hut and addressed Jahangast:

'O great fakir Jahangast! Why do you draw back now? Why are you afraid of approaching? I have tied only one unclean pig at my door. But what you have tied outside the gates of your heart is worse: anger, pride, greed and jealousy. What are you going to do about those pigs rolling in the slime within you?'

At these words of Kabir Jahangast grew ashamed of himself. He realized his folly, says the legend, and became Kabir's disciple.

Kabir has a very well-celebrated song about 'fakiri', the heart and mind of a real fakir.

Mann laago mero yaar fakiri mein
Mann laago mero yaar garibi mein

Jo sukh paaya naam bhajan mein
Vo sukh naahin ameeri mein

My mind's taken to fakiri
My heart's absorbed in simplicity

The bliss I've experienced in meditation
Can't be found in wealth or prosperity.

Kabir is a true iconoclast in the sense that nothing is too sacred for him, except the truth, known experientially. And so, in another very famous song, Kabir dares even to speak in the voice of God. He speaks as if God is talking to man, asking him why he does not feel or recognize what is so close to him.

Moko kahaan dhoondhe re bande
Main to tere paas mein

Na teerath mein, na moorat mein, na ekaant nivaas mein
Na mandir mein, na masjid mein, na Kaabe Kailash mein

Where are you searching for me, O man?
I'm here, right next to you.

Neither in the holy place, nor in the idol
Nor am I in solitary habitation
Neither in the temple, nor in the mosque
Nor am I in Mecca or Mount Kailash.

But Kabir was an iconoclast not only in the sense of questioning others and breaking their precious self-images; he also relentlessly questioned himself. His interrogation is directed at himself as well. After all, his mind is as human as everyone else's. This quality of self-interrogation is crucial if one is not to become self-righteous and blind.

> Bura jo dekhan main gaya, bura na milya koi
> Jo tan khoja aapna, to mujhse bura na koi

> I set out in search of evil
> I found no one bad
> When I looked within myself
> No one worse than I.

Kabir says critics are useful. They point out the truth, even if inconvenient. Instead of silencing or suppressing critics, one in search of the truth would welcome them.

> Nindak niyare raakhiye, aangan kuti chhavaaye
> Bin saabun paani bina, nirmal kare subhaaye

> Keep a critic close
> Shelter him in your house
> Without soap or water
> He cleanses your insides.

Kabir is par excellence a practitioner of the interrogative mode. He questions many of the values that we as a society hold dearest. And it might surprise us how much the same compulsions drive us now as they did in Kabir's time.

For instance, take speed. In our times, especially, the faster a thing is, the better it is held to be. From modes of communication to modes of transport, everything needs to be quick, quick, quick, faster, faster,

faster. Kabir, on the other hand, advocates learning from nature, being in tune with creation, and therefore, slowness, patience, rhythm.

> Dheere dheere re mana, dheere sab kuchh hoye
> Maali seenche sau ghada, ritu aaye phal hoye

> Slowly, oh heart, slowly
> Everything happens slowly
> The gardener may pour endless water
> But the fruit appears only in season.

Or take another great value of our times (and also of Kabir's time, evidently): winning. We are familiar with phrases such as 'the winner takes all' or 'be a winner' or 'victory is all that counts'. We roll back and forth, up and down, on the pendulum of victory and defeat. Kabir, on the other hand, encourages us to learn to lose.

> Kabira tu haara bhala, jeetan de sansaar
> Jeete ko jam le jaayega, aur haara Hari ke dwaar

> Kabir, you're better off losing
> Let the world win in its races
> The winner is carried off by death
> While the loser lands at Hari's doorstep.

What does Kabir mean by learning to lose? Might it mean the ability to surrender, to trust, to not rely entirely on one's own ego and aim exclusively for one's own benefit, even to the detriment of others?

Then Kabir challenges another holy cow, or holy horse, or holy cat. This is the bug of being clever, being smarter than others, being the most worldly-wise. Kabir in fact recommends the opposite.

Kabir aap thagaaiye, aur na thagve koi
Aap thage sukh oopje, aur thage dukh hoi

Kabir, cheat yourself
But never cheat another
Cheating yourself brings happiness
Cheating others brings sorrow.

This seems so counter-intuitive that it takes a while to really grasp what Kabir might be trying to say. Even then, the meaning of a doha or a song tends to reveal itself slowly, over time. To cheat oneself here means, perhaps, the ability to let go, to not be attached, to not grasp, especially as opposed to the all-too-human impulse to envy and avarice, which make us constantly take or appropriate what is not ours.

Another challenge to conventional values thrown up by Kabir (he is relentless!) is the challenge to greed, or the fetish for 'more'. More is good, more is always better, the more the merrier, etc. Kabir, on the other hand, links this constant desire for more with worry.

Chaah gayi chinta miti, manva beparvaah
Jisko kachhu nahin chaahiye, so hi shehenshah

Desires gone, and worries with them!
The mind is now carefree
She who longs for nothing
Is the true emperor of the world.

Kabir points here to an unexpected connection—that desire and worry are two sides of the same coin. You cannot have one without the other. He, on the other hand, has liberated himself of both.

Another legend from his life illustrates this very clearly—how he undermined his own reputation in order to avoid the conventional hankering for fame or success.

The Legend of Licentiousness

Once upon a time Kabir's popularity grew to such an extent that he himself got fed up of it. People were constantly showing up at his door, at every time of night or day, and asking for his 'blessings' or some boons. No one was willing to listen to his actual words when he kept repeating:

Kabir Kabir kya karo, socho aap shareer
Jo tan khoja aapna, to aapahu daas Kabir

Why all this chant of 'Kabir', 'Kabir'
Search within your own self
When you look into your own body
You will be Kabir yourself.

But the hordes of 'followers' kept coming and interfering with his work and his practice. Kabir apparently did have a few dedicated students, including his own children. But he was not interested in setting up a big and bustling ashram, unlike some modern 'gurus'. So Kabir devised a scheme to defame himself.

Kabir approaches a nautch-girl or courtesan well known in the city. He has an unusual job offer for her. He doesn't want any gratification from her, only some well-rehearsed acting. He suggests that they go around in the city together one evening, while he would pretend to be drunk and to flirt with her. She agrees. Kabir chuckles to himself: Let's see how many of my so-called followers remain after this!

And so the spectacle is enacted for the benefit of the residents of Varanasi. They behold the supposedly saintly Kabir walking arm in arm with a courtesan through the market, taking swigs from a bottle appearing to contain alcohol. The pandits and mullahs snigger and exclaim, 'I told you so!' The news spreads like wildfire. And soon Kabir is rid of the chaff among the hordes that were dying to 'follow' him. He returns to his own peaceful life. One man who was narrating this story to me once put it rather colourfully: Only one in a hundred remained.

What we see here is a willingness on Kabir's part not only to break the accepted social icons but to shatter his own public image as well. He did not spare himself! He did not pretend to be holier than others. He certainly did not want to acquire a huge number of fatuous 'followers'. I wonder what Kabir would have made of the 'social media trends' and 'influencers' of our own day!

Root-Idea: Ulat | Upside Down

Das Kabir ki ulti baani
Barse kambal, bheeje paani!

Kabir's language is upside-down
Blankets rain, while water gets wet!

Kabir ki baani atpati, aur jhatpat lakhi na jaaye
Jo jhatpat se lakhi le, va ki khatpat hi mati jaaye

Kabir's words are strange and absurd
You can't get them in a jiffy
Those who get them in a jiffy
Their troubles are over in a jiffy.

'Ulat', or the idea of upside-down, seems entirely natural in Kabir. How could it be otherwise? Things we consider 'normal' are entirely absurd from the mystic's point of view. Our obsession with the world, our thraldom to our senses, our habitual violence, our inability to understand each other, the madness of a world where some starve and others have their mouths stuffed, where some exploit and others are exploited, all this should make no sense even to ourselves.

On the other hand, the things that Kabir speaks about seem incomprehensible to us. He speaks of a reality beyond the senses, of an ability to look and love beyond one's own nose (which we would admit we don't possess, if we were to be honest), of an entirely other way of being. Which way is up, and which way down? What is really absurd and what is 'sensible'?

Working with riddles, paradoxes, animal figures, strange images and symbols, and reversals of what would be considered 'normal', Kabir's poetry entertains and instructs through bewilderment, confusion and absurdity. Or perhaps the poetry is simply designed to baffle. Maybe Kabir is just having some fun! While we seriously try to 'make sense of things'.

Pehle to guruji ham janmya, peechhe bada bhai
Dhoom dhaam se pita re janmya, sab se peechhe maai

O wise one, I was the first to be born
Then my elder brother
With great fanfare my father was born
In the end, my mother.

≈

Chaalega panthi, thaakega baata
Sovega dokariyo ne ghorega rang khaata

Traveller walks
Path gets tired
Old woman dozes
Her bright bed snores!

≈

Agni kahe mane taat padat hai, paani kahe main pyaasa

Anaaj kahe mane khudiya laagi, ghirat kahe main rookha

Fire says I've got the shivers
Water says I'm thirsty!
Grain says it's getting hungry
Butter says I'm dry.

The impossibilities described so casually, mischievously and almost gleefully seem to be telling us that the usual order of things must be turned upside down in order for the truth to emerge, or that real understanding comes only when the 'normal' mind ceases to function. Kabir seeks to strike us dumb—making us lose our 'ordinary mind', our moorings in a habitual, normative way of seeing.

Why is the 'usual' way of looking so terrible? Is it because it is conditioned, unthinking, mechanical? Is Kabir simply having fun or pointing to something more? Or both?

The 'ulatbaansi', or upside-down verse or language, traces its roots in an older tradition called 'saandhya-bhaasha', or twilight language. This language belongs to neither day nor night, and so it does not deal in simplistic categories; it speaks rather of an in-between realm of symbols and significations, alluring and enigmatic at the same time. The saandhya-bhaasha is associated with the Tantric schools of both Buddhism and Hinduism, and also with yogic literature. It is often described in these traditions as a secret communication between guru and disciple, or between initiates, intended to keep lay people out, to prevent them from appropriating, distorting or misinterpreting this esoteric knowledge.

So there was an established tradition of speaking in reversals and riddles that Kabir inherited and then infused with ever greater vitality. Yet scholars have developed vast systems of correspondences, mental categories and meanings to explicate the symbols used in this language (precisely what the mystics may have wanted to avoid!). Thus it is possible to find tables where we will be told 'exactly' what 'lion' stands for or 'rabbit' stands for or 'father' or 'mother' stand for in an 'ulatbaansi'. But if the mystics wanted us to consult tables, why would they compose poetry?

In Hatha Yogic practices, the idea of 'ulat' or reversal seems to refer to an inversion of the usual flow of energy. Energy in a 'normal' human being is described as constantly flowing downward and being dissipated. The entire practice is geared towards causing it to move up towards the higher chakras or energy centres, resulting in enlightenment. This is also characterized as 'ulti Ganga'—the river flowing upstream, in the opposite direction.

But the origins of 'ulat' could be less esoteric than that. Kabir scholar Hazariprasad Dwivedi cites passages from a compilation of 'Gorakhnath's principles' to elucidate a very simple reason behind the necessity for reversal: Our way of life is all upside down. What is most important is given the least priority. What should be first is pushed to the last.

For instance, among the four goals of existence ('purusharthas'), namely, dharma-artha-kama-moksha (duty-wealth-desire-liberation), 'moksha' or liberation is placed at the very end. Or among the four prescribed estates of human life, brahmacharya-grihasth-vaanprasth-sanyaas (celibate-householder-wanderer-renunciant), the search for truth is relegated to the last place, fit only for one's old age. Or take the 'navarasas', the nine moods, in which 'karuna' and 'shanti' (compassion and peace) are placed at the end, and 'shringaar' and 'haasya' (romance and comedy) at the beginning. Gorakh on the other hand insists that what is most valuable must be accorded the most pre-eminent place. And therefore the contrariness towards accepted values.[6]

'Ulat' poetry can be read at many levels: as an outright humorous or funny description of ridiculous impossibilities, with many animal characters thrown in, all for a good laugh; as a code in which the initiated communicate with each other or through which a tradition of knowledge is handed down; or, as the use of language to go beyond language, by twisting or inverting the logic of words to enter a realm that lies beyond this logic.

Kabir asks:

> Dharti to roti bhayi, aur kaaga liye hi jaaye
> Koi poochho apne guru se, vo kahaan baith kar khaaye
>
> The earth turned into a piece of bread
> The crow is flying away with it
> Go ask your guru
> Now where is he going to sit and eat it!

Such questions have no real 'answers' in our terms, because they require an entirely different way of seeing. One where the wolf and the lamb shall feed together and drink from the same pool of water, to take a Biblical image.

> Jab lag sinh rahe ban maanhi, tab lag yeh ban phoole naahin
> Ulta siyaal sinh ko khaai, tab yeh phoole sab banraai
>
> As long as the lion rules the jungle
> The jungle cannot flourish or prosper
> When the jackal devours the lion instead
> The whole forest blossoms and thrives.

What is the 'real meaning' of something like 'the path gets tired because the traveller walks on it', or 'the jackal devours the lion'? There are no ready answers. What lies beyond the realm of sense and logic must be intuited, experienced and lived, not merely conceptualized. The mind must take a leap—and jump off! Perhaps the mind is the lion which needs to be devoured.

You cannot bring a heavy hand to this 'ulat' poetry. The songs are meant to delight. While we ponder and plot after 'meanings', children jive to this poetry instantly! Kids could not be less bothered about meanings or codifications. They are simply thrilled by the joy of reversals and unexpectedness. I have experienced this personally in sharing this poetry with children. Their first response is always sheer delight. There is no evidence of their being daunted by the 'obscure' poetry. On the contrary, to them this poetry seems crystal clear and full of many meanings. And the more meanings there are, the more possibility, the more delight.

This is perhaps close to the mystic's mind—where meanings are direct, unmediated by thought, and unexpected. What, after all, can be the surprise if, in such a paradigm, fish are found to be climbing all over a tree? All answers are to be found in one's own body.

> Jhaad chadhanta machhiya re dekhi,
> sasle sinh ko daraaya
> Keedi kunjal se ladwa re laaga,
> kaun jeeta kaun haara?
> Thaari kaaya mein!

> I saw fish climb up a tree
> A rabbit scared a lion
> An ant wrestled with a crane
> Who won, who lost?
> In your body!

7

Facing Persecution

~

As mentioned earlier, Kabir made a few enemies in his time. When a certain segment of the population lives off exploiting others, in subtle or gross ways, and if someone denounces the exploitation and its agents, it never goes well for the denouncer. Businessmen, particularly corrupt ones, don't like their businesses (or their corruption) being attacked. Those in power do not appreciate being questioned. Those in positions of authority will defend their authority no matter what. With honourable exceptions, this seems to be the general state of human affairs, since time immemorial.

That is why it is often dangerous to speak the truth. The famous Sufi, Mansur al-Hallaj, was hanged for his words in the tenth century. Mansur proclaimed, 'Ana al-Haq', that is 'I am Truth' or 'I am God'. He refused to retract his statement even in the face of threat of death. Even earlier, and in another culture, Socrates preferred to drink from the poisoned chalice rather than compromise on truth or on truth-speaking. In a culture full of falseness, speaking truth is a hazardous enterprise.

Kabir not only spoke the truth, as he saw it, he spoke it uncompromisingly. Fariduddin Ayaz Qawwal, a Sufi singer from Karachi, Pakistan, calls Kabir a 'nangi shamsheer' (a naked sword). He says: 'Kabir spared neither the temple nor the mosque. He attacked all falsehood.'

Kabir's biting sarcasm must have been tough to handle for all the holy men that he attacked. In one song, he attacks the so-called 'yogis' and compares them to an ass, a goat and a bear (for smearing ash on their skin or growing beards or growing dreadlocks). His point is that their focus seems to be on what they can do to the body rather than where the real problem lies—the mind.

Jogi, mann nahin rangaayo, rangaaya kapda

Jaai jangal, jogi, dhooni lagaayi
Raakh lagaayi ne hoya gadhada

O yogi, you dyed your robe ochre
But did not transform your mind

You went to the forest
You lit the holy fire
You smeared yourself with ash
Now you look like an ass!

Kesa kya bigaadiya, jo moonde sau baar
Mann ko kaahe na moondiye, ja mein vishay vikaar?

What harm did your hair do to you
Why do you keep shaving your head?
Why not shave your mind instead
Which is full of hankering?

Jogi jugat jaane nahin, kapda ranga to kya hua?
Mann ka kufar toota nahin, qalma padha to kya hua?

O yogi, you don't know the right approach
So what if you coloured your cloth?
The heresy of your heart is intact, O qazi
So what if you loudly avow your faith?

These were revolutionary words, full of fire, posing a direct challenge
to the authority of the Hindu and Muslim holy men (pandits, yogis,
sadhus, mullahs, qazis). They all tried to hit back hard, as shown in
the following legends.

The Legend of the Encounter with the Emperor

Fed up of Kabir's constant attacks on them and his relentless
mocking of their practices and hypocrisy, the pandits and the mullahs
of Varanasi work up a massive joint petition against Kabir, accusing
him of sedition and of destabilizing the faith and therefore the state.
(Sounds familiar?) They take this petition to the emperor of Delhi
at the time, Sikandar Lodhi, who is camping with his entourage near
Varanasi, and implore him to take urgent action.

They impress upon Sikandar Lodhi the clear and present danger posed by this unruly troublemaker to the prevailing religion and politics of the state. Sikandar Lodhi promptly summons Kabir to his provisional court.

When the royal messengers arrive at Kabir's hut with the summons, he asks them to wait a bit. And then a bit more. And then a bit longer, keeping them hanging till the evening. Then, at last, he presents himself at the emperor's court.

The emperor is furious at being kept waiting. The petitioning pandits and mullahs add fuel to the fire. How dare this lowly creature keep the emperor of Delhi waiting? The nerve of the scoundrel!

In a rage, the emperor asks Kabir to explain himself.

Kabir says that he was delayed by his fascination with an unusual sight.

The emperor begins to get curious instead of angry.

'What amazing sight was it that made you keep an emperor waiting all day?' he asks.

'I was watching a string of camels pass through a street narrower than one's little finger,' Kabir replies.

'Preposterous!' exclaims the emperor. 'How can such a thing be? You're uttering absurdities.'

'O emperor,' says Kabir, 'think of how great the distance is between the earth and the sky and how many camels and elephants and birds and other creatures and things are contained in this space. And all of these things pass into the mind through the pupil of the eye, which is narrower than one's little finger. Isn't this a wonder worth beholding?'

The emperor is strangely impressed by Kabir's enigmatic response and is inclined to consider him a man of uncommon wisdom.

As he is about to let him go, the petitioners, sensing that they are losing their advantage, quickly intervene.

'O emperor,' one of them shouts, 'pay no heed to this impostor's foolishness. In fact, he is a *kaafir*, an unbeliever. Being a Muslim he chants the names of Raam and Hari and says that they are the same as our mighty Allah. What he says is not only ridiculous but also dangerous. Please prosecute him. The only punishment for blashphemy is death!'

Confronted with these strong words, the emperor looks at Kabir. 'Are you a kaafir?' he demands.

Kabir responds with a doha:

Kabir soi peer hai, jo jaane par peed
Jo par peed na jaanta, so kaafir be-peer

Kabir says, only he is truly wise
Who knows the pain of another
He who knows not another's pain
Is directionless, the real heretic.

The emperor lets Kabir go.

But Kabir's trials at the hands of the emperor do not end here. Legends describe another encounter between Kabir and Sikandar Lodhi, of a much more dire nature.

The Legend of the Three Executions

Similar to the previous story, Kabir is summoned to the emperor's court at the petition of various power brokers describing him as a heretic and/or a seditionist and insurrectionist.

In this version, Kabir is brought tied and bound by an armed guard before the emperor.

When he arrives, Kabir stands calmly in front of the emperor, looking him in the eye. Astonished at his insolence, the emperor's ministers command him to bow before the emperor.

Kabir refuses point-blank, saying that he bows only to his true master who is *Alakh*, the Invisible, not to any human potentate.

Kabir is instantly condemned to death. The execution is planned in the traditional style. There are three attempts on Kabir's life, one after the other.

In the first instance, a huge fire is prepared in the middle of a courtyard and Kabir, bound in ropes, is hurtled into the big blaze.

The fire burns and dies out at last. The ministers and petitioners search eagerly for Kabir's remains in the ashes. Instead, they hear the astonishing report that Kabir is back at his hut, calmly weaving.

In the second instance, Kabir is tied in iron chains loaded with weights and thrown into the river. Kabir sinks out of sight. The executioners are now sure that this is the end of the troublemaker. Instead, they hear the next day that Kabir is at his loom, weaving and singing as always.

In the third instance, Kabir is placed in a small inner courtyard, and a mad elephant is let loose from his cage. The elephant trumpets and sways around. He spots Kabir in a corner and rushes towards him. The emperor and the entire court watch from the gallery with bated breath. As the elephant gets closer to Kabir, however, he begins to slow down. As he draws up to Kabir, he calms down completely and sits meekly by his side. Kabir affectionately rubs the elephant's trunk with his hand.

And then Kabir addresses his amazed audience:

'Is there an elephant more mad, O emperor, than a mind that is out of control?'

The historical Kabir may or may not have met the historical Sikandar Lodhi. These stories are obviously the stuff of legend. But they point to how Kabir must have faced persecution during his lifetime. Speaking truth to power, as we said earlier, is a hazardous enterprise, then as now. Perhaps there were attempts on Kabir's life. It is reasonable to suppose that he may have been banished from Varanasi for a time. In fact, towards the end of his life he chose to leave himself.

The courage, in the face of danger, to continue to speak from one's conviction is what is brought home to us in these legends. And this courage belongs to one who is truly fearless. This fearlessness comes in some sense from the recognition of one's own true nature.

What is one's own true nature? We speak now of the mythological figure of the 'hamsa', or 'hans', that is, the swan.

Root-Idea: Hans | The Swan

Ud jaayega hans akela ...

The swan will fly away alone

This is one of the most well-known lines of Kabir in the modern era, delivered hauntingly in the voice of the legendary classical singer Pandit Kumar Gandharva. But who is the swan? Where will it fly to?

The 'hans' or 'hamsa'—swan or, strictly speaking, goose (but mostly translated as swan)—is a bird well-enshrined in Indian mythology. Most intimately, 'ham-sa' represents our own breath— the outgoing and incoming breath. It is an inversion or continuation of 'soham', representing inhale ('so') and exhale ('ham'), which literally translates as 'Thus I am'. So, the word onomatopoeically represents the individual or the self or the soul.

Many legends have accrued around the figure of the 'hans', and its characteristics are traditionally described as follows. The swan lives on Mansarovar lake, near Mount Kailash. It is reputed to have the ability to separate milk from water even when the two are mixed. For its food, it eats only pearls (not fish) and drinks only milk (not water). Its white colour is a symbol of purity, as is its abode high in the mountains.

In Hindu mythology, the 'hans' is also the 'vehicle' of the Goddess of Learning, Saraswati. Its diet consisting only of pearls ('heera' or 'moti') is typically contrasted to that of the 'bagula' (heron/stork) which eats fish. Its ability to separate milk from water, and drink only the milk, represents an extremely important spiritual quality—discrimination ('vivek'). It is said to be able to live in water without its feathers getting wet (rather like the lotus), therefore symbolizing worldly engagement and yet perfect detachment. Its white plumage symbolizes spotless virtue. Its flight can be taken to represent liberation from the cycle of samsara.

The bird is said to be migratory, dwelling on Lake Mansarovar in the summer, and leaving it for the plains in the winter. So, one recurrent motif uses this as an allegory for the human condition—the 'hans' leaves Mansarovar, its true abode, and flies down to the plains, a land of shallow puddles and ditches. It forgets its way back to the high mountain lake. Gradually, it forgets where it came from. It even forgets that it is a swan. It starts to eat fish and to drink water from shallow puddles.

Mansarovar refers to the real lake in Tibet next to the holy mountain Kailash (said to be the abode of Shiva). It derives its name from the combination of the words 'manas' and 'sarovar' (mind and lake). It is supposed to have been conceived in the mind of Brahma. It represents the ocean of pure consciousness, which gives birth to the material world.

Mansarovar Lake is even today a place of pilgrimage for people of many faiths. Drinking its water or bathing in it are held to be powerful acts of cleansing and purification. In Hatha Yoga, since the seventh or crown chakra is also known as (Mount) Kailash, Mansarovar then comes to represent the pool of nectar ('amrit') which lies next to it. This 'amrit', held in an inverted well near the top of the head, confers immortality. The swan has to find its way back there somehow.

All these images form a powerful cluster—the bird who flies alone, the pure, great lake that is its home, and the pearls and milk that form its diet. This symbolic universe comes together repeatedly in the poetry of Kabir and other mystic poets, and strikes a powerful chord. When the Bhakti or even Sufi poets (for example, Shah Latif of Sindh) evoke the image of the 'hans', they are drawing on a well-established and ever-evolving tradition. Kabir says famously:

Ud jaayega hans akela,
jag darshan ka mela

The swan will fly away alone
The world, a mere carnival of sights.

Kabir evokes an ultimate aloneness, ever present at all moments, that we all sense and feel. Perhaps 'death' brings this home most starkly. The swan, like a ruby or a true seeker, is not found in big crowds or numbers.

Laalan ki nahin boriyaan, hansan ke nahin paat
Singhan ke nahin lehere, aur sadhu na chale jamaat

Rubies are not found in sackfuls
Swans don't move in flocks
Lions are not found in herds
And a true seeker walks alone.

This existential aloneness is not depressing. It is empowering. It is simultaneous with an existential relatedness. There is only One—all 'others' are also 'I', and vice versa. In another place, Kabir says:

Ham sab maan, sab ham maan,
ham hain bahuri akela

I am in all, all are in me
I am many and alone.

There is a repeated exhortation in Kabir to taste our own essential being-ness (paradoxically found in 'death') away from all our attachments, connections, hankerings and bonds. There is a powerful call to us to fly back to our true abode.

> Chal chal Mansarovariye, unvar hanso khel kare
> Jaage jyot jadohariye, chetan choon chuge

> Come, let's go to Mansarovar lake
> Where the swan is at play
> Roused by a sparkling light
> The swan pecks, aware and awake.

There is equally a description of our dilemma of being in the world. As the swan spends a period of time here, it tends to forget where it came from. And so, the 'hans' gets lost among the 'bagulas' (herons). The real spiritual work, as many traditions affirm, is to remember our 'true nature', which we have somehow forgotten.

> Ochhi talaai bug ghano, avsar aayo hans
> Mat kar talaai gaarbo, tu samdarvaasi hans

> The pond is small, swarming with storks
> Now is your opportunity, O swan!
> Don't mess around in this puddle
> You're a native of the ocean, O swan!

The swan comes from a *vast* place, a place of spaciousness, wider and broader than the petty calculations of the ego. This is what we seem to have forgotten. We are all swans walking around as if we were crows.

When it remembers, and is ready, the swan reaches Mansarovar without wings. It arrives without having to fly there, indicating that this deep pool of consciousness, of nectar ('amrit'), literally lies within. In one song Bananath, a nirguni poet of the oral traditions, says:

Sahaj sarovar simrath hansa, par bin kiya re piyaana
Mansarovar moti chugta, nirmal neer nivaana

The swan remembers the lake spontaneously
And reaches there without use of wings
It eats the jewels of Mansarovar
And bathes in its clear waters.

The jewel or pearl that the swan eats is a figure for the outer or inner food that we take in. Everything is *aahaar* (food)—what we eat, air, environment, thoughts and impressions. Where are we engaging our attention, or what are we consuming? The 'heera' that a true swan picks out is described in several songs by Kabir. In one song he calls it the 'Name'—that is, the sound that reverberates within, which often takes the form of a mantra for a spiritual seeker, and which connects us with the universal sound.

Hove re bhaag bhala saadho
Satguru maliya, padiyo samand maan seer
Hansa re hove chug leejiye
Naam amolak heer

My fortunes improved, the stream merged
Into the ocean, when my true guru came

If you're a swan, then eat only
The precious jewel of the Name.

Sometimes the swan arrives as a long-awaited guest. One's recognition of one's own true self can be long in coming. The moment of meeting one's own swan-soul is a sacred one. The swan has come as a beloved guest to grace this house, a figure for the body. It is an essential encounter with oneself—the ending of illusion and the welcoming of something more real.

Aaj to hajaari hanso paavano
Mhaare aaj to kaaya ro raajo paavano

Today the swan is my special guest
Today the king of this body is my guest.

8

A Philosophy of Love

~

KABIR could be called a poet of biting social satire. He could be called a devotional poet (in the nirguni tradition). He could be called a poet of death (given how often he invokes death in his poetry). But he is also par excellence a poet of love. Kabir is all these things.

Love forms a cornerstone of Kabir's philosophy and poetry. Love *is* the point. The biting social satire is to indicate the lack of love in our social hierarchies and institutions. The devotion (to Raam, Hari, Allah, Alakh) flows from a foundational fount of love. Death—the kind that Kabir recommends—*is* love. Love arises with the death of the small, limited ego.

> Yeh to ghar hai prem ka, khaala ka ghar naahin
> Sheesh kaat bhoun dhare, tab baithe ghar maanhi

> This is the house of love
> Not your favourite aunt's house!
> Cut off your head, put it on the floor
> Then you may enter the house.

In fact, Kabir is quite blunt. To not be able to love is really to be dead, to have missed life entirely. As long as we are devoid of love, we are actually lifeless.

> Ja ghat prem na sanchare, va ghat jaan smashaan
> Jaise khaal lohaar ki, jo svaans let bin praan

> Those in whom there is no love
> They are like cremation grounds
> Like the bellows of an ironsmith
> They breathe without life.

In one striking song, Kabir describes the entire loveless world as dead. He says, 'Saadho, yeh murdon ka gaaon' (Seekers, look, this is a village of the dead). All the inhabitants of the village are dead, the king, the subjects, the doctors and the priests, even the sun and the moon are dead. Only in love there is life.

But what *is* love? Everyone talks about love. Our whole culture is obsessed with it, producing endless romantic films, songs and literature about it. The idea of love dominates our consciousness. But do we understand what love is?

Kabir defines love quite clearly.

> Prem prem sab koi kahe, prem na cheenhe koi
> Aghat prem pinjar base, prem kahaave soi

> Everyone talks about love
> No one knows what love is
> Unwavering love, which dwells within
> That is called love.

In other words, real love is something that properly belongs to us. It doesn't depend on circumstances. It doesn't become 'less' or 'more' according to the situation. It doesn't increase when conditions are favourable ('Oh, I love you so much!') and decrease when there is some pressure or stress ('Oh, now I'm not so sure!'). It is that which is constant, steady, one's own. It is within one's own body. This love is autonomous, not circumstantial. It has been earned, it is not a fluctuating attribute of an unsteady mind, now less now more.

> Prem piyaala so piye, jo sheesh dakshina de
> Lobhi sheesh na de sake, vo naam prem ka le

> The drink of love is for one
> Who can lay down her head
> A greedy person can't give up her head
> Though she may chant the name of love.

This state of love exists beyond the thinking mind, beyond the self that divides, which *thinks* it knows. This mechanical mind—the heavy head—must be given up in order to taste the wine of love. Love is much higher than, superior to, intellectual knowledge. It is another dimension altogether. It is rooted in another paradigm of knowledge—an experiential knowledge of the true nature of the self and of the world.

That is why Kabir, unlettered himself, is scathingly critical of mere book knowledge. Knowledge, in the theoretical, intellectual sense, is not higher than love, in Kabir's vision. It is in fact much lower.

> Padhi padhi ke patthar bhayo, likhi likhi bhayo hai eent
> Kahe Kabir tohe prem ki, laagi na ekai chheent

Reading endlessly, you've become a stone
Writing endlessly, you've become a brick
Kabir says, not one drop of love
Has touched your skin.

Experience is the ground of true love, not theories, books, information or intellectual jargon. This cannot be emphasized enough. This love must be *tasted*. It must be experienced. It must be felt and lived within one's own body. There is no point in writing or reading tomes about it, if one has never known it oneself.

Likha likhi ki hai nahin, aur dekha dekhi baat
Dulha dulhan mil gaye, to pheeki padi baaraat

It's not a matter of reading and writing
It's a matter of experience
When the bride and groom meet in union
The wedding party is of no significance.

It is our choice. Do we want merely to be part of the wedding party, speculating idly on the nature of love and union—or do we want to taste it ourselves?

Kabir is insistent about the nature and experience of love. He holds it to be the highest station, the highest dimension that human beings are capable of. It is far more important than cleverness, something we set so much store by in our time (and perhaps it has been so at all times—socially, 'smartness' outweighs love). It is a far more fundamental human element than our pathetic pride, our attempts to bolster our constantly crumbling, fading 'self-esteem'. It is something far more empowering. It is the potent fuel for the voice of utter confidence in which Kabir always seems to speak.

Haman hain ishq mastaana
Haman ko hoshiyaari kya
Rahein aazaad ya jag se
Haman duniya se yaari kya

I'm drunk on love!
Why be clever any more?
I'm free of this world!
Why be worldly-wise any more?

Chaakho chaahe prem ras, raakho chaahe maan
Do khadag aur ek myaan, dekha suna nahin kaan

Either keep your precious pride
Or get a taste of love
Two swords in a single sheath?
No one heard of such a thing.

And Kabir can feel and describe this experience of love with so much tenderness, so much persuasiveness, that you cannot help but be moved. Who would not want a taste of this tender, heart-expanding, beautiful experience?

Nainon antar aav tu, naina jhanp tohe lun
Na main dekhun aur ko, na tohe dekhan dun

Nainon ki kar kothri, putli sej bichhaaye
Palkon ki chik daar ke, piya liya rijhaaye

Come into my eyes, my love
I'll shut my eyes and hold you close
I won't look at anyone else
Nor let you look elsewhere

Make your eyes a room
Make your pupils the bed
Make your eyelids the curtains
Make love to your beloved here.

This arrival of fulfilment is connected to the experience of longing, of the pain of separation, of one's soul searching and yearning to meet and unite with the beloved. This is called *viraha*. The experience of being human, of being without love, of being separate and disconnected from others and from truth or the ultimate reality, is traditionally described in this particular poetic idiom. The lover (typically 'female') is longing for her beloved (typically 'male'). This longing (for the truth, for the divine, figuratively called the 'beloved') is an expression of love and itself leads to love.

Akhiyan prem basaiya, jin jaane dukhdaai
Naam snehi kaarane, ro ro rain bitaai

Nainan to jhari laaiya, rahat bahe nis baas
Papeeha jyon piyu piyu kare, piya milan ki aas

Eyes full of love
This is the cause of grief
In love with the Name
The whole night spent in tears.

Eyes full of love
These tears flow night and day
Like the brainfever bird cries out
Constantly for its beloved.

Love being the most important value, there are constant reminders, both in the poetry and in the legends surrounding Kabir, that intellectual knowledge or academic, theoretical formulations or theories, cannot be held to be of higher account than love. There is a striking legend that seeks to illustrate in its own way the power of Kabir's love. Typically, it pits a learned Brahmin, a professional pandit, well versed in the classical scriptures, arrogant and vain, against the lowly, illiterate, humble weaver called Kabir.

The Legend of Sarvajit

There was once a pandit called Sarvanand. He was well versed in the scriptures and had a great skill for argumentation. He challenged learned pandits to debate in the hoary Indian tradition of 'shastrartha' (scriptural interpretation) and defeated all of them one by one. Once he had achieved his mission of defeating all the greatest pandits in theological debate, he rechristened himself 'Sarvajit', the All-Conquering.

Full of himself and thrilled to bits, Sarvajit came home and announced the news of his conquests to his mother. 'From today onwards, mother,' he said, 'I am Sarvajit. For I have defeated all the learned pandits in debate and am justly renowned as the greatest and wisest Brahmin in the land. You can be proud of your son!'

His mother calmly looks him up and down and replies:

'You may well have defeated all those charlatans in debate. But I will consider you the wisest man if you can defeat Kabir.'

'Kabir? Who is this Kabir? I've never heard of him.'

'He's a weaver who lives in Kashi.'

'A low-caste illiterate weaver! Who are you comparing me to, mother?'

'I will believe that you are the wisest man in this land if Kabir says so.'

'Harrumph!' snorted Sarvajit. 'I will go right now and challenge this Kabir to debate. You just wait and see.'

And so Sarvajit sets out on the long journey to Varanasi. He loads his bullock-cart with all his pothis (scriptures), ready to quote from a hundred authorities in support of his arguments.

As he's nearing Kashi, he spots a young girl by the wayside. He's thirsty and she appears to be carrying water. He stops and asks her for some.

This girl is Kamaali, Kabir's daughter, but Sarvajit doesn't know this. She looks at his mountain of pothis, and the poor bullocks groaning under their weight, and asks him where he's headed.

'I'm going to see Kabir,' says Sarvajit.

'Why?' asks the girl.

'To defeat him in argument and prove to my mother that I'm the most learned one there is. Do you know where he lives?'

Kamaali laughs when she hears of Sarvajit's absurd enterprise, going to argue about scripture with a weaver, armed with a mountain of holy books. She utters a doha, in the guise of giving directions.

Kabir ka ghar shikhar pe, silhali se gel
Paanv na tike papeel ka, kyon pandit laade bail?

Kabir's house is on the mountain-top
And the path up is slippery
Even an ant loses its footing there
Why load your bullock-cart, O pandit?

Sarvajit is furious at this insolence and leaves the girl behind in a huff. In a while, he arrives at Kabir's little hut, amazed that his mother has sent him on a wild-goose chase to this poor abode.

He calls out in a challenging voice.

'Kabir! O Kabir! Come out and face your nemesis.'

Kabir emerges from his hut looking puzzled.

'Yes, brother, how may I help you?'

'Don't call me brother,' snaps Sarvajit. 'I'm here to challenge you to a debate. I am willing to give you one day to prepare yourself.'

Kabir is baffled by this.

'What debate? Why me?' He looks at the manuscripts piled up on the bullock-cart. 'I don't even know how to read or write!'

'Hmph! I thought as much,' says Sarvajit. 'Nonetheless, you must debate with me about theological matters and I must defeat you.'

'But why?' asks Kabir. 'What do you really want?'

'I want proof that I have defeated you in debate.'

'Look, I don't want to have any debate with you or anyone else. Why don't you just say that you have defeated me in debate? You're free to tell everybody this. I won't dispute it.'

'But where is the proof?'

'What sort of proof can I give you?'

'I want it written down and signed by you.'

'I don't know how to write, O learned pandit. Why don't you write it down yourself and I'll put my thumbprint to it?'

Sarvajit is very happy with this simple solution. Promptly he whips out a piece of paper and writes on it: 'Kabir certifies that Sarvajit has defeated him in debate and that he, Sarvajit, is the wisest man of all.'

Kabir promptly puts his thumb on the paper and is glad to be rid of the fired-up pandit.

Sarvajit makes the long way back to his village.

Arriving at his doorstep, he proclaims loudly to his mother:

'Mother, I have come back. And I have defeated Kabir in debate!'

His mother is sceptical. 'Show me the proof,' she says.

Sarvajit digs into the folds of his clothes, brings out the chit that he has prepared himself, and hands it to his mother.

His mother reads the note, smiles, and wordlessly hands it back to Sarvajit.

Sarvajit is puzzled. He takes the note and reads it. It reads: 'Sarvajit certifies that Kabir has defeated him in debate and that he, Kabir, is the wisest man of all.'

Sarvajit is astonished!

'It's not possible,' he exclaims. 'I wrote this myself. It must be a mistake! I must have made a mistake. Wait, I will go back right away and bring back proper proof.'

His mother merely smiles at him.

And so Sarvajit sets out again on the long way to Varanasi. Again he arrives at Kabir's doorstep. One more time he challenges him to a debate, claiming that a mistake had been made the last time. The same sequence of events ensues. Sarvajit is seen off with his triumphant note, duly stamped by Kabir's thumb. Again he arrives at his house and shows the note to his mother. Again the order of names is reversed.

A furious Sarvajit heads to Varanasi a third time! The whole sequence is repeated yet another time. After the third instance, Sarvajit realizes that something strange is afoot. Indeed, his mother was right. Kabir is more wise than he, having 'defeated' him even without having to debate. And so he returns to Varanasi, without his pothis, and becomes one of Kabir's disciples.

This legend illustrates nicely the staunch opposition of the ordinary folk to the 'learned' wiseacre of the Brahmins and pandits. Kabir is invested with magical powers here precisely to assert, as the folk would like to do, that the most important wisdom is beyond scriptural knowledge and learning. Kabir symbolizes that position.

> Vakta gyaani jagat mein, pandit kavi anant
> Satya padaarath paarkhi, birla koi sant

> Speakers, scholars, priests and poets
> Roam the world in countless numbers
> But one who has tasted truth
> That is a rare seeker.

> Kabir pustak padh padh ke, ast pada sansaar
> Peed na upji preet ki, to kyon kar kare pukaar?

> Reading endless books
> The world lies tired and flat
> If you haven't felt the pain of love
> How can you utter a single true word?

For Kabir, it is not a question of whether knowledge is higher or love is higher. That's because, for him, love *is* knowledge. This is a radical conception. Love, as we said, is something that needs to be experienced, not merely theorized or conceptualized. This experience takes place within the individual body. This knowledge, then, is equally available to everybody, within their own body. It is a radically democratic notion. In one blow it does away with all kinds of hierarchies of knowledge.

To gain the ultimate knowledge and to have an experience of love *is the same experience*. This love brings higher knowledge;

higher knowledge releases this love. The two are bound together inextricably. One of Kabir's most famous and most quoted dohas speaks of precisely this.

> Pothi padh padh jag muaan, pandit bhaya na koi
> Dhai aakhar prem ka, padhe so pandit hoye

> Reading book after book, they died
> Not one of them became wise
> Read the four letters of love
> That's how you become wise.

But this love, this knowledge, this wisdom, is not something that can be spoken about too easily or frivolously. Kabir says that it is a deep inner experience, indescribable, unutterable, an 'untellable tale'. And yet, he cannot stop talking about it.

Root-Idea: Akath Katha |
An Untellable Tale

Akath—inexpressible, indescribable, ineffable. Beyond words, beyond language, beyond mind.

Some things or states are simply beyond description in language or speech. Poetry or art may come close; but that is the closest we can get. 'Madness' also comes close. And so, this indescribable state is also compared to madness or intoxication. It is called masti! Kabir calls himself an 'ishq mastana'.

In the modern 'scientific' age, anything outside of sense perception, beyond ordinary description, escaping the bounds of reason, is often held to be unacceptable. Science must be able to measure a thing for it to be true. The mystic worldview is starkly different. It engages with a space that renders one dumb, and groundless. This place is called love.

> Akath kahaani prem ki, kachhu kahi nahin jaai
> Goonge keri sarkara, baithe muskaai

> Untellable is the tale of love
> Beyond words
> Like a dumb man eating sweets
> Smiles silently.

Words bring their own boundaries. Discourse is a bound place. Each time we say something, we are constructing a narrative, which is invariably limited to a particular point of view. It reveals a partial truth. In order to stitch together a coherent narrative, one that shores up our favoured conclusions and convictions, we reinforce certain truths and conveniently forget others.

> Had mein baitha kathat hai, behad ki gam naahin
> Behad ki gam hoyegi, tab kuchh kathna naahin

> Settled within limits, you discourse
> With no inkling of the limitless
> When you glimpse the limitless
> No more need for words.

This couplet draws attention to the common etymological roots of 'kathna' and 'kehna' (storytelling and speaking). Perhaps the untold tale, that lies beyond language, allows us to intuit a space holding multifarious points of view as one integral experience.

And so Kabir keeps 'saying' what cannot be said. He goes on urging, challenging, mocking and exhorting us using words, even while insisting that words are not enough.

In the song 'Maya Maha Thagini' Kabir lays out all the forms taken on by perceptive reality. What are the forms of attachment ('maya')? For Vishnu, it's Kamla, for Shiva, Parvati; for a pandit, it's the idol; for the pilgrim, it's the holy water; for a king, it's the queen; for some, a diamond, for others, a couple of coins. In the end, he says:

> Bhaktan ke bhaktin hoi baithi, Brahma ke brahmaani
> Kahe Kabir suno bhai saadho, yeh sab akath kahaani

> For devotees, it's their devotion
> For Brahma, his creation
> Kabir says, listen seekers
> All this is an untellable tale.

Here, the tale's indescribability seems to lie in the paradox of how reality is one and yet manages to take on so many diverse forms. This cannot be understood by our usual, logical, dualistic, linear and categorical ways of thinking. And therefore, it cannot be described in those terms.

In another song, Kabir describes a boat that has finally started sailing smoothly. This boat has no fear of shallow waters, nor of deep ones; even if it were to overturn, no harm would come to the traveller. This boat can bear the weight even of a mountain, because the true guru has charted out its path. In the end, Kabir says:

> Kahe Kabir jo bina sir kheve, so yah sumati bakhaane
> Ya bahu hit ki akath katha hai, birla khevat yeh jaane

> Kabir says, one who rows without a head
> That boatman alone can speak this wisdom
> It's an indescribable tale of great benefit
> Only a rare boatman knows it.

Stories of headless boatmen are obviously not within the bounds of realism! They lie somewhere beyond conceptual understanding. Perhaps this is the point at which Kabir starts to speak the unspeakable language ('yeh baat hai nirbaani'), the 'ulatbaansis', upside-down or nonsense-verses, which tell of fish growing on branches of trees, or rabbits that have turned into hunters, or the ant who's carrying an elephant and a camel off as her dowry.

What really is sense, or sanity, or reasonableness? If we were to think in the upside-down terms of the mystics, we are asleep when we think we are awake, and we are mad when we think we are sane. Madness is sanity; sanity is madness. Are we unwilling to admit that we live in a world gone mad?

The spiritual experience in many traditions is described in terms of intoxication. It is called bewilderment, exhilaration, folly. To be drunk; to be high; to be utterly absorbed or lost; to lose one's senses... To stray from the 'ways of the world'. To finally stop being 'normal', or even 'rational'. (And then no 'sense' can be spoken.)

To experience another dimension, one must go beyond this one. The word 'ecstasy' has its roots in the Greek word 'ekstasis'—to cause to stand outside. Outside of what? Outside of oneself. Trapped in the prison of one's small mind and daily self, how do we cause ourselves to stand outside?

Love is an intoxicating thing. It is tinged with madness, or what the world calls madness. It goes against everything we have been taught in the school of worldliness. Sensible people have a rightful fear of love. It can destroy everything the 'reasonable' self holds dear.

Mystics, on the other hand, fear only a state of no-love—a cleverness, or worldliness, which is akin to prison or death.

To be alive and free in this sense is to be liberated from the cold and sensible calculations of 'less' and 'more', 'gain' and 'loss', 'mine' and 'yours'. An iconic Kabir song says this:

Halki thi jab chadhi taraazu
Poori bhayi phir kyon tole?

Feeling small, you climbed the scale
You're full now, what's there to weigh?

This song also has the very interesting metaphor of one's individual awareness ('surat') as a bartender! The idea perhaps is that we are constantly serving our wine to others—trying to impress, trying to score points in others' eyes in order to feel good about ourselves, trying to find validation through others. But finally this bartender, this wine-maker, has got drunk on her own wine. She has stopped serving it to others.

> Surat kalaalan bhayi matvaali
> Madva pi gayi antole

> My awareness, the bartender, has got drunk
> She gulped down her own wine.

The refrain of the song says it all (pun intended).

> Mann mast hua, phir kya bole?

> My heart and mind are drunk
> What's left to say!

Ideas and words go only so far. This journey seems to point to the other end of them, where only experience can reach. An unknown Sufi poet describes (in words) the wordless experience of love.

> Ab lafz-o-bayaan sab khatm hue
> Ab lafz-o-bayaan ka kaam nahin
> Ab ishq hai khud paighaam apna
> Aur ishq ka kuchh paighaam nahin

> Now words have come to an end
> Now there is no more need of words
> Now love is its own message
> And there is no message of love.

At this elemental juncture, experience speaks its own language. No more tales to tell.

9

The Universe Within

~

ANOTHER cornerstone of Kabir's vision is the continuum of 'without' and 'within'. 'Baahar bheetar sakal nirantar', as he says. Outside and inside the same, unbroken reality. Like water flowing through a porous material; or light passing easily through a glass jar. The human being is not a solipsistic, solid, unbreachable box, dark inside, totally separate from the external universe. Instead, the human being reflects the outer world in her own inner structure. The two are one reality.

This is the classical idea of the microcosm reflecting the macrocosm, found in both Eastern and Western thought. As above, so below. Kabir says:

Khel is brahmaand ka jab pind mein dekhiya
To jag ki bharamna sab door bhaagi
Baahar bheetar ek akashvat hai
Tahaan ulti dor kar sushamna laagi

When I saw the play of the universe
Within this body
All delusions about the world
Dropped away.

Outside and within
The same unbroken space
I reversed the central thread
And pointed it upwards.

This is why the body is of central importance in Kabir. The universal play can be glimpsed *within the body*. While the body is not the self, the body is the site of experience. And only this experience can reveal and confirm the true nature of the self. Without experience, one speculates; with experience, one knows. Several classical Indian traditions of spirituality have tended to denigrate the body in order to emphasize the difference between the body and the self. Kabir too attacks the identification with the body in some of his poetry. But, overwhelmingly, he gives the body a central importance as the crucible of the most crucial knowledge there is.

Ya ghat bheetar saat samandar
Ya hi mein nau lakh taara

Ya ghat bheetar anhad garje
Ya hi mein uthat phuvaara

Dhoondhe re dhoondhe andhiyaara

In this body, all the seven oceans
And the nine million stars, in this body

In this body, the sound of the universe
And fountains of elation, in this body

Yet you search in the dark!

Kabir's point is that the light is within us, and it can be felt, seen, experienced and known *in the body*. What we're seeking is to be found right here. And yet, we insist on looking in the darkness.

This is how universal knowledge is possible. Because it is of the size of the body, not an ungraspable, unfathomable expansion of space. It is not got at through mental exertions. It is arrived at through plunging into the body.

And this reality resides in *every* body. ('Ghat ghat mein panchhi bolta'—the same bird sings in each and every body.) And so this potential, this possibility, is entirely democratic. It is available in equal measure to everybody. It is not reserved for those higher in the social hierarchy, for those with access to books or teachers, for those who have acquired any kind of intellectual knowledge through any means. It is the most democratic, equitable faculty there is—the potential of a human being to discover his or her true nature. And how vast this nature is! And how petty our limited self-conceptions and our small minds, in comparison.

It is with this backdrop that Kabir repeatedly urges us to stop 'wandering outside' in search of fulfilment and 'look within' instead.

Kai dhoondhti phire tu mhaari heli?
Mat bhaagti phire tu mhaari heli

Ghat ghat mein Raam ji bolein ri!
Parghat piya ji bolein ri!

What are you looking for, dear friend?
Don't keep running, oh my friend
Raam resides in every body
In every body, the beloved sings!

Because our search is entirely misplaced, it feels fruitless and neverending. A thing lost in one place cannot be found in another. An anecdotal story about Rabia of Basra tells of how she was absorbed one evening, as darkness fell, in looking for something under an oil lamp hanging from a tree in the village square. One man stopped to ask her what she had lost. She said, the key to her treasure chest. The story spread through the village in no time. Rabia has a treasure chest! To which she's lost the key! Soon the whole village gathered under the tree to help her in her search. At last, one person wisened up and asked Rabia where exactly she had lost the key.

'In my house,' she said.

'Then why look for it here!' exclaimed the villagers.

'But there is no light in my house. I can't look there. Here there is light from the lamp. I can look.'

'But, Rabia, that's absurd! How can you expect to find something in one place when you lost it in another?'

'But isn't this what you also do?' Rabia countered. 'You lost something inside your house, yet you keep looking for it outside!'

Because of our senses—our power to see, to hear, to interact with the external world in a variety of ways—we feel that there is 'light' outside and darkness within. But can the torch beam of the mind be pointed inward? Can we shine the spotlight within?

Kahe Kabir kya kho gaya, kya dhoondhan-haara?
Andhe ko soojhe nahin, thaara ghat maan hi ujiyaara

Kabir asks, what have you lost, friend
And what are you looking for?
The blind man does not realize
The light is within his own body.

Kabir uses the traditional figure of the 'eighty-four lakh yonis', endless animal and creature births, or repeated births and rebirths, to indicate this fruitless and eternal wandering, looking for something elusive, an endless search. Like the traditional figure of the musk deer who keeps searching in the forest for an aroma that is emanating from itself.

Kasturi kundal base, aur mrig dhoondhe ban maanhi
Aise ghat ghat mein Raam hai, moorakh samjhe naahin

The musk lies in its own sac
Yet the deer hunts for it in the forest
So Raam resides in every body
Fools don't get this.

And yet, the right kind of wandering can be a welcome sign of detachment. Traditional Indian systems urge everyone to leave the householder's life, its pleasures and its duties, around the age of fifty, by which time they are supposed to have relieved themselves of all worldly responsibilities. Kabir himself is reputed to have wandered all over the country. In his later years he may have been a solitary, wandering figure, part of a timeless stream of spiritual travellers in a well-worn Indian tradition. An allegorical legend—but one which relates to a very real tree, still existing—speaks of his possible journey to Gujarat in western India.

The Legend of the Banyan Tree

Once upon a time there lived two brothers by the name of Tatva and Jeeva. The names are significant. Tatva symbolizes the universal essence; and Jeeva stands for the individuated self.

In their youth they have a premonition that they must await the arrival of their guru. But how will they recognize the guru? The two brothers plant a dried banyan root at a central spot in their courtyard. Whenever a sadhu or a holy man is passing by, they welcome him eagerly and wash his feet at this spot. In spite of repeated watering in this manner, the buried banyan root remains dormant.

This lasts for about forty years, at the end of which period they are on the verge of giving up. One day an ordinary-looking man happens to arrive at their hut, asking for water. They make him sit near the spot in the courtyard and out of habit wash his feet, not expecting anything. The man drinks the water, rests for a while and then continues on his journey.

The next day, the two brothers notice a fresh, young sprout of banyan from the spot! Immediately, they remember the man whose feet they washed the previous evening. They remember asking his name. 'Kabir,' he had said. They promptly set out in search of Kabir and adopt him as their guru.

At that spot, which is in Gujarat, a huge banyan tree stands even today, and the place is known as 'Kabirvad' (Kabir's Banyan). A Kabir song from Malwa, alternatively ascribed to another poet in the tradition, Shivguru, speaks about the symbolism of roots:

Gura to ji ne gyaan ki jadiyaan dai
Va jadiyaan to mhaane laage pyaari
Amrit ras ki bhari

Call him a guru
Who gives the roots of wisdom
I am enamoured of those roots
Full of a healing nectar.

Who is the guru who plants and nourishes the roots of wisdom,
who brings the seed of the big banyan bursting out into life? In many
places, Kabir says it is the Word itself, 'Shabd', or Universal Sound,
vibrating within us.

Root-Idea: Surat–Shabad | Awareness and the Word

> Shabd kahaan se uthta, kaho kahaan ko jaaye?
> Haath paanv va ke nahin, phir kaise pakda jaaye?
>
> Naabhi-kamal se uthta, shoonya mein jaaye samaaye
> Haath paanv va ke nahin, vo surat se pakda jaaye
>
> From where does the Word arise?
> Tell me, where does it go?
> It has no hands or feet
> Can one catch it or no?
>
> From the navel-lotus it rises
> Into emptiness it goes
> It has no hands or feet
> Awareness can catch its flow.

The idea of the Word is found across many religious and mystic traditions. In the Abrahamic religions, it refers to the Word of God, from which creation sprang. Speech is one of the essential attributes of God. There is the Biblical idea of the Word becoming flesh, and the Qur'an is held to be a physical manifestation of God's direct words to his Prophet.

In nirgun Bhakti traditions, 'shabd' has a very strong connotation of sound. The word is always sound first, and only later its 'meaning'.

Word in the primordial sense is pure sound. Sound is vibration, the fundamental fabric of the entire universe. The whole of creation rests on sound.

One of the terms often used for this is 'anaahat naad' or 'anhad naad', that is, 'unstruck' or primordial sound. It is 'unstruck' in the sense that this sound is not made by any human hand or material means; on the contrary, this sound is what brings all of creation into being.

The impact of this word, this powerful sound, on the listener is often described as *chot* or wound in Kabir's poetry. This wound is not merely 'being moved' or 'feeling transported' in the usual sense. It's a palpable, visceral, transformative experience, which affects you in ways that hurt. It is like the philosopher J. Krishnamurti claiming that the very brain cells are altered in a moment of authentic understanding. Something shifts. It is not always a 'pleasant' experience. It is an experience of transformation.

> Ghaayal ki gati aur hai, auran ki gati aur
> Jab prem baan hirday laga, tab raha thikaane thor

> The gait of a wounded one
> Is different from that of others
> When struck by the arrow of love
> You find your true abode.

And therefore, in Kabir the word is often envisioned as an arrow (shabad vaalo baan), a weapon that cuts or pierces through. The vulnerability that comes with being penetrated is described as shabd ki chot (the wound of the Word). This is the principal weapon in the armoury of the guru, used by him or her to wound you, to strike 'you' (your ego, your sense of a separate self) down. The guru is a hunter out on the hunt.

So many songs of Kabir in the oral traditions use militaristic sounding metaphors—arrows, cannons and shields—but in a way that subverts the ordinary understanding of war and aggression.

> Koi maare top teer se, aave dwaadas ghaav
> Mera satguru maare shabad se, tal mundi ne upar paanv

> Some strike with guns and arrows
> Your body is covered with wounds
> My true guru strikes with the Word
> The world is turned upside down.

And what changes and shifts in you when you're struck, wounded, when the crust has been pierced, the mask broken through? Everything falls apart—the whole personality changes—new perceptions arise—the world is turned upside down. Finally, you begin to experience something more than your small, limited self.

> Tu kya jaane peed paraai
> Shabad ki laagi hoye to jaanajo mere bhai
> Bhajan ki laagi hoye to jaanajo mere bhai

> What do you know of the pain of others?
> Unless you've been struck by the Word
> Unless you've been struck by song.

In another instance, Kabir speaks in riddles, as he often does, with reference to the Word. The realm of the Word is a mysterious place, outside of our usual markers.

> Shodhun shabad mein kanihaari bhai
> Dhoondhun shabad mein kanihaari

Bina dor jal bhar kuen pe
Bina sees ki vo panihaari

I look and search, oh friend
For the secret in the Word
Of the riddle of the headless water-girl
Drawing water from a rope-less well.

Kabir singer Mahesha Ram Meghwal from Rajasthan says that the
Word is a secret communication between the seeker and the guru,
particular to that seeker, given to him particularly by his guru. He says
that Shabd is not one but two, pointing to his two nostrils, indicating
that remembrance of the breath, its incoming and outgoing, is the
deeper meaning of 'Shabd'.

This is reflected in a well-known Kabir song, 'Koi Sunta Hai Guru
Gyaani' (A Wise One Listens).

Oham soham baaja re baaje, trikuti shabad nishaani
Ingla pingala sukhman joya, shvet dhwaja phehraani

The drums of inbreath and outbreath resound
I aim for the Word at the three-peaked summit
Where left, right and central channels meet
And plant my flag of victory there.

The 'three peaks' are where the three yogic energy channels—Ida,
Pingala and Sushamna—meet. These channels run with the breath
up and down the spine. They unite at the centre of the forehead, the
'third eye chakra'.

There are two key ideas to grasp about 'Shabd'—one, that it is
formless, or 'pre-creation'; and second, that the individual awareness,

'surat', must merge with this formless sound from which all of form (or creation) arises. So, Shabd is in a sense the cornerstone of the 'nirgun' (beyond form) tradition. It is in contradistinction to the 'sagun' (with or in form) tradition, which emphasizes the image or the idol, and the particular attributes of a deity. It emphasizes sound as opposed to form, hearing as opposed to sight. No wonder this tradition is primarily oral, and depends highly on the faculty of 'listening'. And so, Kabir's constant exhortation—*Suno!* (Listen.)

If the nirgun tradition has a 'deity' or a sense of the supreme, it is Shabd. That is why it is also called the 'Shabd parampara' (tradition or way of the Word). Shabd is the ultimate guru. Shabd is also the final destination where the individual attention (surat) must make her way.

Brahma re Vishnu Maheshwar deva, teenon aava to gaman
re
Us akshar ko laghu na maatra, vohi shabad rata kar re, hansa

Brahma, Vishnu and Shiva
All these gods come and go
But that letter which is neither long nor short
Meditate on that Word, O swan.

To abke dhyaan dharo mere bhai, phir yo avsar nahin aai
Kahe Kabir suno bhai saadho, shabad mein surat milaai

So meditate now, my friend
This moment won't come back again
Kabir says, listen seekers
Merge your awareness in the Word.

Surat (not to be confused with 'soorat', the common Hindi/Urdu word for 'face') may be described as the most intimate thing one has: one's attention, or awareness, or consciousness. In a sense, it represents the individual self. It is also called 'surta' or 'surti', and is commonly conceptualized as 'female' (yearning to unite with the 'male' beloved, that is, Shabd).

This is distinct from *mann,* or the mind. One's attention can be caught up in the mind (that is, in thoughts), or it can be free of the mind. It is important to recognize that awareness and mind are essentially different. Several poems make it clear that 'surat' is distinct from both body and mind.

> Tan matki mann jherna, surat bilovanhaar
> Maakhan Kabira kha gaya, chhaachh piye sansaar

> Body the pot, mind the churning-stick
> Awareness, the one who churns
> Kabir ate up all the butter
> The world's content with buttermilk.

Kabir is extremely sceptical about the mind, or 'mann', and constantly derides its unsteadiness, its avariciousness, its general unreliability. The mind is not to be trusted.

> Mann lobhi, mann laalchi, mann chanchal mann chor
> Mann ke mate mat chaaliye, mann palak palak mein aur

> The mind's greedy, the mind's avaricous
> The mind's unsteady, the mind's a thief!
> Don't follow the ways of the mind
> It changes every moment.

Awareness has to extricate itself from the clutches of the grasping, flickering, fluctuating mind. 'Surat' is etymologically related to smriti, or simran, that is, remembrance. Simran and meditation are synonymous in several Indian traditions. That is, meditation in the sense of awareness of self, or self-remembering. In this state, the self is released from the grasp of the thinking mind and remembers itself. The self becomes aware of itself. Awareness begins to cognize itself. Consciousness becomes truly conscious. The 'seer' becomes the seen. There are many, many ways to say this ...

The central thing here is 'surat', that is, the individual awareness. There is constant talking to the 'surta' in this tradition. The 'surat' has to be cajoled into spiritual practice and meditation.

> Mhaari syaani surta
> Mhaari laadli surta
> Raam ras pyaalo jhel ri
> Raam naam tu bol ri
> Antar ka parda khol ri

> O my artful awareness
> O my darling awareness
> Fill your cup with the wine of Raam
> Have Raam's name on your lips
> Rend the inner veil.

Kabir is frequently talking to or heckling the 'surat' (mostly to mend its ways). The upshot seems to be that this dratted 'surat', our attention, keeps getting caught up in outer distractions, and is therefore constantly led away from itself. The point is to cultivate stillness, to pin down the compulsively roving attention.

Surta phansi sansaar mein, yahaan se pad gaya door
Surat baandh kar sthir karo, to aathon peher hazoor

Awareness got entangled in things
This caused an alienation
Bridle the attention and make it still
Then the Lord is always with you.

Surat is sometimes clubbed with *nirat,* or absorption, that is being without awareness of individual self. *Surat-nirat* may be read together in the sense of awareness with a self to 'have' it, and pure awareness without a self.

In a beautiful song, the seeker is addressed as a bird who wanders from forest to forest. The last verse speaks of what is to be done with this precious jewel, one's attention.

Panchheeda bhai, heera vaali haata mein
Teri maala ra motida bikhrya jaaye
Surta mein nurta po le re
Ban ban kyon dole re?

O fellow bird, in this jewellers' market
Your pearls are getting scattered
Weave your awareness on the thread of emptiness
Why wander from forest to forest?

The moment when the fluctuating consciousness finally arrives into stillness is an amazing, inexpressible one.[7]

Tan thir mann thir vachan thir, surat nirat thir hoye
Kahe Kabir va pal ko, kalp na paave koi

Body still, mind still, speech stilled as well
Attention and absorption still
Kabir says such a moment
Is beyond conception!

When the wandering attention finally heads home in order to find its place of rest, it discovers that its true abode is 'Shabd', the Word. The mysteries of the universe reveal themselves when this happens.

Chanda na deekhe chaalta, badhti na deekhe bel
Saadhu na deekhe sumarta, yeh kudrat ka khel

Chanda deekhe chaalta, aur badhti deekhe bel
Saadhu deekhe sumarta, surat shabad ka mel

The moon can't be seen moving
The creeper can't be seen growing
The seeker can't be seen meditating
This is nature's way.

See the moon moving
See the creeper growing
See the seeker meditating
When awareness merges in the Word.

One popular and lovely metaphor that features 'surat' prominently is that of the divine wedding. Awareness is seen as a young woman or girl, who's out to seek a groom. This adventure, if it goes well, ends in an elaborate wedding ritual, culminating in the night of union.

Ghano rhijhaayo vo laadli ne, ghano rhijhaayo ji

Yo var paayo vo deewaani ne, yo var paayo ji
Mhaari surat suhaagan naval bani, saahib var paayo ji

She wooed him well, that dear, crazy girl
And what a match she has found
My awareness has become a new-wed bride
And the groom is the lord himself.

The recurring metaphor is one of union—where the bride of awareness must lose herself at last, and find a greater reality waiting for her. But which way must she go to find her beloved?

The 'surat' must climb into the sky ('gagan') to merge with the 'Shabd'. This is a way of describing the yogic process of reversing the flow of energy, usually flowing 'downward' (through the chakras) and out, making it go 'upward' instead (to the top of the head). The point in the 'sky' where the three rivers meet ('triveni') or where the three peaks combine ('trikuti') is where this merger takes place. Ida and Pingala are the left and right energy channels representing duality. When they combine with the central channel, Sushamna, at the third eye chakra, in the yogic system, that's when we glimpse this other, greater reality. That's when the bride meets her groom, Radha her Krishna, Shakti her Shiva, Surta her Shabad. Finally there is the peace and bliss of union.

Naam ratat mann sthir bhaya, gyaan kathat bhaya leen
Surat shabad ekai bhaya, jal hi ho gayi meen

Remembering the Name, the mind was stilled
With words of wisdom, it became absorbed
Awareness and Word united
The fish dissolved into water.

10

Defiant in Death

~

DRAWING close to the end of his life, Kabir lost none of his fire or his iconoclasm. Kabir lived most of his life in Kashi, or Varanasi, the holy city. Even today, people from across India come to Varanasi to die, because it is held in the Hindu tradition that if you draw your last breath in this holy place you go straight to heaven. A sort of visa and passport to paradise! These days the small town of Maghar, near Gorakhpur, is not so well-known. But in those days, Maghar was reviled (especially by the 'pure-bred' of Varanasi) as a foul and disgusting place, fit only for the worst. This may have been because it was primarily inhabited by Muslim weavers and other 'low-caste' people. It was claimed that if you died in Maghar, you would be reborn as an ass.

So there was already this dichotomy between Varanasi and Maghar, a direct toss-up between heaven and hell, or the life of an ass. One, the ideal place to die; the other, to be avoided at all costs, in life or in death. So what does Kabir do? He says, I lived all my life in Varanasi, but I'm going to Maghar to die. He deliberately leaves Varanasi and goes to Maghar at the end of his life! Never short of throwing a challenge, our man. He is supposed to have died there, and has a shrine dedicated to him which is visited by many people. He has transformed in some measure those old superstitious beliefs associated with Maghar.

Kabir challenged the simplistic heaven-and-hell narrative of his time. He questioned the mainstream, accepted belief that one place is good to die and another place isn't. What are the widely accepted, simplistic narratives of our own times? Is it that one ideology is better than another? That one kind of view is more virtuous than another and therefore everyone must hold the same view? This, in my view, is the best way to relate with Kabir—to question the orthodoxies of our own times.

With his actions, not just his words, Kabir asked the basic, logical question: Do the fruits of our life depend simply on where we managed to die, instead of how we actually lived our lives? And so Kabir, defiant even in death, goes to Maghar, to make the point that it is the quality of your life not the site of your death that counts.

> Kahai Kabir sunahu re santon,
> bhram pare jin koi
> Jas Kaasi tas Magahar oosar,
> hirdai Raam sat hoi

> Kabir says, listen good people
> If you still don't get it
> As Kashi by the river,
> so arid Maghar
> The two are identical once Raam
> has occupied your heart.

And the fact is that Kabir didn't die. He became everybody. He lived up to his name, Al-Kabir, the 'Great'. He lives, even today, in the minds, hearts, tongues and songs of the people of this land. Kabir is alive and well and continues to speak the truth loudly and confidently in a thousand tongues. He still brings courage to millions of marginalized, oppressed or disempowered people who draw strength from his words, and contribute their own words to this grand poetic tradition called 'Kabir'. And that's why he lives today, lives perhaps more vitally than we who are 'alive'.

Or, in another sense, Kabir died much before his death. That's why he couldn't care less about dying in Maghar or in Varanasi. He was already dead to all such concerns. Several spiritual traditions speak of the need to 'die before one's death' or 'dying while still alive'. What does this mean?

Could it be pointing to the need to die to a false idea of the self? In order to wake up to a larger reality?

What is the 'self'? Is it just the bundle of hopes, fears, desires, regrets, plans, calculations, that we carry around inside us? If so, would it be so terrible to die to it?

Mann mari mamta mari, mar mar gaye shareer
Aasha trishna na mari, keh gaye daas Kabir

Minds have died, affections died
Body after body has suffered death
Hope and desire have still not died
So states Kabir.

Kabir speaks often about the need to 'die before death'. He is ready and prepared for physical death because he has already embraced it while alive.

Jo marne se jag dare, so mere mann anand
Kabahu marihun, kabahu paaihun, pooran paramanand

That death which the world fears
Brings joy to my heart!
When will I die, when embrace
The bliss of wholeness?

Kabir attends the approach of death with joy in his heart instead of the usual human reaction of fear. This is because he has mastered the 'art of dying'. Death, too, is an art to be mastered, a skill to become proficient in. It is the work of a lifetime. We have our whole lives to do it. Put bluntly, one must know how to die. That is how one begins to live.

Marta marta jag muaan, mar bhi na jaane koi
Aisi marni mar chalo, phir na marna hoi

The world dies death after death
No one knows the art of dying
Learn to die in such a way
That you never have to die again.

This 'dying before death' is paradoxically the genesis of an experience of true love. Love can be true only when it is born of the ashes of the death of personality, the small ego, the self-cherishing, self-insistent 'I'. To die to oneself brings about this expansion, this space, this liberation of the heart, which is necessary in order to taste the drink or the fruit of love.

Kabir bhaati kalaal ki, bahutak baithe aaye
Sir saunpe soi piye, nahin to piya na jaaye

Kabir, many are those who visit
The winemaker's distillery
Only those who pay with heads may drink
This drink is not for others.

~

Ooncha taruvar gagan phal, aur birla panchhi khaaye
Va ko to vo hi bhake, jo jeete ji mar jaaye

Tall tree, sky fruit
A rare bird eats
Only that one can reach it
Who dies while still alive.

This is why death is often celebrated and hailed in Kabir's poetry. This kind of death is liberation—freedom from a small, limited, isolated, self-absorbed self, tied like a dog to the ups and downs of life, now happy, now sorrowful, now ecstatic, now in agony.

An evocative image of death that comes repeatedly in Kabir's verse is the figure of the pearl-diver, called marjeeva, which means 'one who lives again after dying' or 'one who is reborn in death'. The pearl-diver plumbs the depths of the ocean, and resurfaces (is born again) with the pearl (of wisdom or insight) in his hand—a perfect metaphor for the idea of 'dying to live'.

Main marjeeva samudra ka, dubki maari ek
Mutthi laaya gyaan ki, ta mein vastu anek

I'm a pearl-diver
Plunging into the deep

I bring back fistfuls of wisdom
Countless shining pearls.

Thaara bharya samand maan heera, marjeeva laaviya
Thaara ghat maan hi gyaan ka zanjeera, saahib suljhaaviya

Your ocean is filled with pearls
A pearl-diver will fetch them up
Knowledge is tied up in your body
A Master will undo the knots.

We cannot honestly talk about life without taking death into account. Even in small, everyday ways, we face constant deaths. Friendships die, relationships end, marriages and businesses fall apart, monuments crumble, children leave home, success turns into failure or fame into irrelevance, and old ways of living inevitably come to an end. How we face death—these smaller deaths or the ultimate, big one (or the many deaths after many births)—determines how well we live our lives. And vice versa—the better we live our lives, the more prepared we are for death.

Kabir keeps reminding us relentlessly of the fact of death. This is necessary because we keep forgetting. It is astonishing how many songs about death there are in his repertoire. Perhaps it is a way to wake us up from our overweening sense of arrogance and invincibility. We, who imagine we are so great, will be swept away by the winds of time, as many before us.

Chun chun maati mahal banaaya, moorakh kahe ghar mera
Na ghar mera na ghar tera, hai jagat mein phera

Khaak mein khap jaana re banda, maati se mil jaana
Nahin karo abhimaan, ek din pavan sa ud jaana

Laying brick upon brick
The fool says, 'My house'!
Not my house, nor your house
This world's a merry-go-round.

You'll turn to dust one day
You'll merge with the earth
Don't be so proud, oh fellow
The wind will blow you away.

Kabir says that we live lives of forgetfulness, unmindful of the overwhelming reality of death, which may come at any moment. Each moment is potentially the moment of death but we live our lives as if we are immortal. And so, when death comes, often unexpectedly, we are not prepared. We must be prepared for death in each moment because death is always just one moment away.

Kabir gaafil kyon phire, aur kyon sove ghanghor
Tere sirhaane jam khada, jyon andhiyaare chor

Kabir, why wander forgetfully
Why this deep sleep of unawareness?
Death stands by your bedside
Like a thief hides in the darkness.

When we are prepared to meet it, death is our friend. Perhaps the most famous and celebrated story about Kabir's life is the story of his death. Kabir's paradoxes never cease to amaze or astound. Even in death, Kabir eludes the grasp of those who would pin him down.

The Legend of the Flowers

When Kabir is nearing his death, both Hindu and Muslim followers gather around him in Maghar. When he dies, the fighting begins. Was Kabir a Hindu or a Muslim? Should he be cremated or buried? Should they prepare a pyre or a grave for him? Both sets of 'followers' want to claim Kabir's dead body and his legacy. They would like to do the final rites according to their own beliefs even though Kabir himself, throughout his life, persistently criticized this unthinking attachment to ritualism. Hindus insist that Kabir should be cremated and his ashes dispersed over the Ganga. Didn't he always sing of 'Raam' and 'Hari'? Muslims insist that Kabir should be buried and a shrine erected to him over the spot. Didn't he take birth and live in a Muslim household? Meanwhile, the body lies covered in a white shroud.

This is the way of the world. We will kick the living saint, persecute and harass him, throw stones at him, put him on the cross. After his death we will sanctify him and glorify his image. A dead saint is more useful than a living one! Why? What drives us to revere the dead more than the living?

There is a version of the story, which I like, in which Kabir himself appears, resurrected like Christ. He comes to the crowd gathered round his dead body and innocently asks someone what is going on. When he is informed of the dispute, he asks them whether they're sure that this is Kabir's body at all. The followers are outraged at this insinuation. The stranger asks them to lift the shroud to check.

When the shroud is lifted, there is no body. Instead, there is a bundle of flowers occupying the space where the dead body had been.

Then the solution is simple. The flowers are equally divided. Hindus take half the flowers and perform the cremation with the right ritual chants. Muslims take the other half and bury them and erect a mazaar to the saint.

But I often wonder, when I think about this story, did any of them—did anyone present among all those who arrived at such a satisfying practical solution—did any of them actually take in the fragrance of those flowers? Did they breathe in Kabir's spirit? Did anyone absorb the essence and not just pay obeisance to the crust?

I hope that in this book, through the life and poetry of the phenomenon called Kabir, I have been able to give you at least a whiff of that essence, the spirit of Kabir, which endures and is alive even today.

Root-Idea: Shoonya | Emptiness

Shoonya, literally zero in the Indian numbering system, is the place from which all things begin. It is the origin, the source, the womb. In Sanskrit, one of its primary meanings is empty space or void. It is also a term in Buddhist thought, usually translated as emptiness or nothingness.

To our modern minds, any talk of emptiness may feel rather frightening. After all, we do tend to fill our lives up with as many things, events and people as we possibly can. A single empty moment in our social-media-fuelled lives can feel threatening. But for Kabir 'shoonya' is the abode of most fulfilment and restfulness. The emptiness that he experiences and conveys is liberating instead of frightening or depressing.

In several of his poems, Kabir talks about his 'des', his land, the country where he comes from. Where is Kabir's country? It is nowhere. What landmarks does it contain? It contains nothing. Kabir empties out the universe, evoking an experience and a self free of the limitations of form.

> Amaare re des maan nahin dhara, nahin gagana
> Nahin koi pavan na paani
>
> Amaare re des maan nahin chanda, nahin sooraj
> Nahin koi navlakh taara
>
> In my land there's no earth, nor sky
> No wind, nor water

In my land there's no sun, nor moon
No nine billion stars.

Further on in this song, he dismisses Brahma, Vishnu and Shiva, he puts away the Gita and the Vedas, he eliminates all rising and setting, all birth and death. Kabir is cleaning out of view all that we cling to for meaning. All our usual markers of understanding, of 'making sense' of the world, of what we consider 'important', are undermined. He evokes a place beyond dualities, where radiance, or illumination, showers without cause, where there is one without a second. He is pointing to a subtle reality beyond, or behind, the obvious one of forms, which we call our world.

Sakhiya va ghar sabse nyaara,
jahaan pooran purush hamaara

Jahaan nahin dukh sukh, saach jhooth nahin
Paap na punya pasaara
Nahin din rain, chaand nahin sooraj
Bin jyot ujiyaara

Friend, that house is most marvellous
Where my Complete One dwells

No grief or joy, no truth or falsehood
No good or evil there
No day or night, no sun or moon
Without a flame there's radiance there.

Kabir constantly dismisses 'night and day' from our ken. Night and day stand for all the dualities that we live among and that we are subject to. The land of freedom is beyond these dualities. Kabir says this country cannot be reached by foot (or any other mode of transport). It has no habitation, nothing that is recognizable. If we could orient ourselves to this incredible country, we would lose all fear of death.

> Bin paavan ka panth hai, bin basti ke des
> Bina pind ka purush hai, kahe Kabir sandes
>
> A path walked without feet
> A country without habitation
> A person without a body
> Follow these signs, says Kabir.

Kabir has fixed his attention *there*—which is nowhere. Kabir abides in that place—which is no place. He is utterly at home in Shoonya—because he is free of himself. He is utterly unafraid of death—because he is already dead to himself.

> Jahaan na cheenti chadh sake, raai na thehraai
> Mann pavana ki gam nahin, tahaan Kabir lau laai
>
> Where no ant can climb
> No space for even a grain
> No mind or breath exist
> Kabir is absorbed there.

This extraordinary place can be found, can be seen, only if you know the secret of where and how to look. But if you do find this empty place, if you do arrive here, then, paradoxically, there is joy, music, love, celebration.

Mehram hove so ee lakh paave, aisa des hamaara

Shoonya mahal mein baaja baaje, kingri been sitaara
Jo chadh dekhe gagan gufa mein, darsega agam apaara

If you know the secret you can see it
Such is my country.

Drums resound in the palace of emptiness
Lutes, sitars and sarangis
Climb to the steep sky-cavern
And behold the pathless-peerless.

There is an exhilaration to the emptiness. This emptiness is very full.
And joyful.

Shoonya shikhar par anhad baaje
Raag chhatees sunaaunga
Nirbhay nirgun gun re gaaunga

On the peak of emptiness
The primal sound resounds
I'll sing all the sounds
Of the universe

Fearlessly I'll sing
Of the beauties of the formless.

In the Hatha Yogic tradition of the Nathpanthis, 'shoonya' becomes
identified with the seventh chakra on the top of the head, thus also
called the 'shoonya-chakra'. This is where the term 'shoonya-shikhar'

(peak of emptiness) seems to originate, since the crown chakra is also known as Mount Kailash.

Images of heights, of climbing up, of mountaintops, evoke a sense of unfettered, undivided space, which we also understand as a hallmark of the sky. So, often, in these songs, the term 'shoonya-shikhar' is used interchangeably with another very common term, 'gagan-mandal' (the dome of the sky). Both evoke that sense of space near the top of the head where unfragmented sound and light are in free play.

Various metaphors of structures or form are used to describe this experience of formlessness—'shoonya mahal' (palace of emptiness), 'shoonya shahar' (city of emptiness), 'shoonya gadh' (fort of emptiness).

Sunn sahar baas hamaara, tahun sarvangi jaavai
Saaheb Kabir sada ke sangi, sabad mahal le aavai

In the city of emptiness I dwell
A complete one makes it there
Kabir and his lord are together forever
In the palace of the Word.

In an era when the multiplicity of things and forms threatens to overwhelm our minds and senses, these poems celebrate a different kind of wealth—the joys of nothingness. This is the famous fakiri of Kabir. It is not just an outer renunciation—it is an inner letting go of all that binds our mind and heart, all that inhibits a wide and deep understanding. It is a shedding of all ego, pride and arrogance.

Kar guzraan gareebi mein, sadhu bhai
Magroori kyon karta?

Abide in austerity, fellow seeker
Why so much pride?

Kabir's emptiness is an active choice—having less rather than more, having no identity rather than a strong identity. In a culture and mindset of being obsessed with more (more possessions, more wealth, more knowledge, more information, more experiences, more success, more relationships, more gratification, more of 'me' in every way possible), Kabir's voice strikes a markedly different note.

It is up to us whether we pay heed to this voice or not, whether we listen from our emptiness to what he's shouting out to us from his emptiness.

Suno bhai saadho!

Note on Translations and Transliteration

~

T HE songs and dohas of Kabir are found in a wide variety of shapes and forms in different textual and oral sources. Often there are several different versions of the same poem, with slight or large differences in the arrangement of words or verses or in the words themselves. Drawing upon on all the sources that I'm personally aware of, oral and written, I have chosen as my text for translation the version, or a combination of versions, which appealed most to me personally. Like all extant Kabirs, my Kabir too is a personal one, at the same time as being very much part of a broad and deep tradition.

Additionally, having space for a limited number of poems, I have selected the ones that seemed to me the most striking, representative or popular, often being all three at the same time. The poems here represent the tradition as a whole and are not limited by purported notions of authenticity as works of a single, historical figure. In the selection of both the songs and the dohas, I have focused more on the oral Kabir, that is, the poems attributed to Kabir that have become the most quoted and used by ordinary, everyday people who preserve, perpetuate and make up this tradition. There were many poems it was difficult to leave out, but I'm happy with the ones that do occupy this space. Broadly speaking, I have organized the selection of songs and dohas in the following manner.

Beginning with some of the most classic songs and dohas attributed to Kabir, proceeding to the savage poetry of mockery for which Kabir is so well-known, to poems specifically about a seeker's practice as Kabir sees or recommends it, poems about the guru, to verses delineating a strange, upside-down world, to songs of universality, joy, love and longing, to stark poems about death and mortality, typical of Kabir, and ending in some of his most esoteric and mysterious poems. These are not hard-and-fast divisions for, indeed, all poems cross over from one such artificial category into another. But this is a rough chart of the organising principle that I have followed here.

The transliteration policy followed throughout for representing the poems in the original has been a rough-and-ready one, a kind of intuitive system used by most Indians in their daily navigation of the linguistic dichotomies they inhabit. The choice to not use a more formal and academic and often forbidding diacritical system of representation of the Devanagari script is a deliberate one.

Sixty Iconic Songs of Kabir

I'M DRUNK ON LOVE

I'm drunk on love
What need of cleverness?
I'm free in this world
What need of worldliness?

They wander who are lost
Parted from the beloved
My beloved dwells in me
I have no hankering

Not once did I lose sight of him
Not once did he leave my side
I'm constantly connected to him
I have no uneasiness

The world strives for fame
Such struggle to make a name
The guru-given name is truth
Why forage for acclaim?

Kabir is drunk on love
His heart free of duplicity
Such a delicate path to tread
Why overburden your head?

Song: Haman hain ishq mastaana

IF ALLAH LIVES IN THE MOSQUE

If Allah lives in the mosque
Who occupies the rest of the world?
If Raam inhabits idols and temples
Why did no one find him there?

They say Hari dwells in the east
And Allah abides in the west
Look in the heart, only the heart
To discover both Allah and Raam

Who says holy books are false?
False is unthinking adherence
Perceive the one in everyone
Kill the fear of the other

Every woman and man ever born
All are embodiments of you

Kabir is the child of Allah-Raam
That reality is my true guru.

Song: Jo khudaay masjid basat hai[8]

Where Do You Keep Looking for Me?

Where do you keep looking for me, O Man?
I'm right next to you

Not in the holy place, nor in the idol
Nor am I in solitary habitation
Not in the temple, nor in the mosque
Not in Mecca or Mansarovar

Not in chants, nor in austerities
Nor am I in ritual fasting
Not in any kind of rites
Not in yoga or renunciation

Not in the body, nor in the life-energy
Nor in the universal sky
Not in between the eyebrows
But in the breath of each breath

If you look for me, you'll find me
In a second's search, in an instant
Kabir says, listen fellow seekers
I reside in the quality of trust.

Song: Moko kahaan dhoondhe bande

THIS CLOTH WAS WOVEN FINE

This cloth was woven fine
Made from the fibre of Raam

What was the warp, what was the weft
With what yarn was woven, this cloth?

Left and right, the warp and the weft
The central channel, the yarn for this cloth

Spun on the loom of eight lotuses
Five elements, three gunas, in this cloth

The creator took ten months to weave it
The pounding of the loom fashioned this cloth

This cloth worn by gods, men, ascetics
All of them made it dirty, this cloth

Humble Kabir wore it with attention
He returned it as he received it, this cloth.

Song: Jheeni jheeni beeni chadariya

ALL THIS SPINNING AND WEAVING

Kabir has quit
All this spinning and weaving
He's inscribed Raam's name
On his body

As long as there is
Thread in the loom
Awareness of Raam
Keeps snapping

Watching this,
Kabir's mother weeps
Oh God, what is this boy
Going to eat?

Call me stupid,
Of a lowly weaver caste
Yet I have earned
The prize of Hari

Kabir says,
Listen, O mother
The lord of the world
Fulfils all needs.

Song: Tanna bunna tajyo Kabir

THE LORD IS A MASTER DYER

The lord is a master dyer
Who has coloured my cloth

He got rid of the dark blots
And put on a fast red hue
Even on washing it doesn't fade
Everyday it grows more true

The vat of feeling, water of tenderness
He soaked it in the dye of love
He scrubbed the dirt of bodily sorrow
And coloured it through and through

The cloth has taken the master's colour
The beloved is skilled and clever
I surrender all I have to him
Body, mind, wealth, the very breath

Kabir says, the dear dyer
Poured his grace on me
Wearing this cool and pleasant cloth
I have found rapture, fulfilment.

Song: Saahib hai rangrez, chunariya mori rang daali

LIFT UP YOUR VEIL

Lift up your veil,
the beloved awaits you
Oh, lift up your veil

In every body, the same sovereign
Why speak harsh words to anyone?

Don't be proud of wealth or beauty
Illusory, this five-coloured cloth

Light a lamp in the palace of emptiness
Be not swayed by winds of desire

With practice and skill, I found him here
In this house, the priceless beloved

Kabir says, here is bliss
The throb of an ancient drumbeat.

Song: Ghoonghat ke pat khol, toko piya milenge

KNOWLEDGE CAME LIKE A STORM

Brothers, knowledge came like a storm!
The curtains of delusion got blown away
Maya could not stay

The twin pillars of duality fell
The beams of misconception broke
The roof of desire crumbled
Pots of misunderstanding shattered

With effort and skill, seekers built a house
Lime washed, impregnable to water
The failings of the body wiped out
When Hari was glimpsed within

The rain that came after the storm
Soaked Hari's lovers in love
Kabir says, the mind was illumined
Like the sun dispels all darkness.

Song: Santon bhai, aayi gyaan ki aandhi

NEITHER RIGHTEOUS NOR UNRIGHTEOUS

I'm neither righteous nor unrighteous
Neither ascetic nor pulled by desire
I don't speak, nor do I listen
I'm neither servant nor master

I'm neither bound nor free
Neither restrained nor indulgent
I don't walk apart from others
Nor do I walk along with anyone

I'm not cast down to hell
Nor do I attain to heaven
All actions are done by me
I'm apart from all action

A rare person understands this
One who has become unshakeable
Kabir says, don't exalt anyone
Nor run anyone down.

Song: Na main dharmi na hi adharmi

CONSTANT, SPONTANEOUS AWARENESS IS BEST

Seekers, constant,
Spontaneous awareness is best
From the day it arose, with the guru's grace,
It has continued without end

No closing of eyes, no blocking of ears,
I don't torture my body
With open eyes, I see and laugh
And enjoy the beauty of form

All speech, a mantra, all hearing, meditation,
My food and drink are prayer
Home and forest equal in my gaze
I've destroyed the feeling of being other

Wherever I roam is a pilgrimage
Whatever I do is service
My sleep is akin to prostration
I bow to no other idol

The ceaseless Word occupies my heart
I've let go of murky passion
I've connected with a timeless beat
Sitting or moving, always unbroken

Kabir says, this natural being
I have expressed in self and song
There's a realm beyond sorrow and joy
That realm brings most joy.

Song: Santon, sahaj samaadhi bhali

It's Hard to Escape Maya

O ascetic, it's hard to escape Maya
You try out a thousand ways
But you can't loosen its hold

You left the house and became a hermit
You left your retreat, and went wandering
You left your children, but took on disciples
Maya envelops you in everything

You gave up lust, but anger got you
You gave up anger, but there was greed
You gave up greed, and the ego got you
You strutted and paraded shamelessly

A desireless heart can quit Maya
Attention immersed in the Word
Kabir says, listen brothers
This wisdom is for a rare seeker.

Song: Avadhu, maya taji na jaai

TALK TO ME OF ANCIENT THINGS

O Swan,
Talk to me of ancient things

Where did you come from, O Swan
And where will you settle?
Where do you find rest, O Swan
And where do you place your hopes?

This is the dawn of consciousness, O Swan
Go with me to that land
Doubt and sorrow don't abide there
Nor the terror of death

Here gardens of delight are in bloom
With their beguiling fragrance
Here the mind-bee gets ensnared
With no hope of fulfilment.

Song: Hansa karo puraatan baat

THE SPIRITUAL PATH IS SUBTLE

Seekers, the spiritual path is subtle

Neither desire nor undesire
Attention fixed in devotion

Every moment spent drenched
In the blissful gush of meditation

Awareness absorbed in Raam
Like fish inhabits water

The head sacrificed in service
Not a moment's hesitation

Kabir says, the path of Bhakti
Was thus given expression.

Song: Bhakti ka maarag jheena re

THE FISH IS THIRSTY IN WATER

Oh seeker
The fish is thirsty in water!
I laugh when I hear
The fish is thirsty in water

Without self-knowledge, you wander
Someone to Mathura, another to Kashi
The deer has musk in its belly
But roams the forest desperately

Lotus in water, petals in the lotus
The bee comes to rest on the flower
So the mind is mastered and expands
For yogis, practitioners and seekers

He whom the three gods contemplate
And countless other yogis
That one sits in your own body
Supreme undying being

What's right here, you call far away
All talk of 'far away' is fruitless
Kabir says, listen seeker
Only the guru can shatter illusion.

Song: Paani mein meen piyaasi

THE HOLY CITY HAS ONLY WATER

The holy city has only water
I've seen all this bathing
Come to nothing

All idols are only stone
For all your entreaties,
Never seen them talking

All holy books are only talk
I lifted the body-veil
And looked with my own eyes

Kabir speaks only of experience
He's seen through
This hollow sham.

Song: Teerath mein sab paani hai

HOW WILL OUR TWO MINDS MEET?

How will our two minds meet?

I speak from experience
You parrot words from a book
I speak words which resolve
You like to complicate things

I say, stay awake
You stay firmly asleep

I say, stay detached
You cling to everything

It's been explained for ages
Nobody wants to practice it
Blundering on a blind path
You fritter your wealth away

The guru flows like a clear stream
Immerse and wash within
Kabir says, listen seekers
Then you may become that.

Song: Tera mera manva kaise ek hoi re?

WHO CARES FOR YOU, O FORMLESS GOD?

Who cares for you, O formless God?
No one serves you, unmanifest deity

They worship idols and forms
Perform all kinds of ritual
The lord is whole and unfragmented
They can't crack this riddle

The heads of Brahma, Vishnu, Shiva
Are thickly coated over with moss
Don't rely on these fellows who
Themselves didn't make it across!

The ten avatars are gods of time
They can't really save us

They're bound to cycles of karma
The real doer is nameless

Yogis, sadhus, ascetics, monks
Bicker idly among themselves
Kabir says, listen seeker
Glimpse the Word, get out of this mess.

Song: Angadhiya deva, kaun kare thaari seva?

WHAT YOU SAY IS ALL LIES

What you say is all lies, O Pundit
What you speak is sheer deceit
If chanting 'Raam' brought salvation
Saying 'sugar' would've tasted sweet

If limbs got burned by saying 'fire'
And crying 'water' appeased the thirsty
If shouting 'food' could satiate hunger
The world would be saved already

The parrot, like his master, chants away
With no conception of Hari's greatness
When the bird flies off to the forest
Hari doesn't enter its awareness

Without direct perception or contact
What will come of chanting a name?
If saying 'money' made one millions
Which poor guy would stay the same?

Your real love is things of the world
You mock those who yearn for Hari
Says Kabir, no love in your heart
In shackles, carted off to death-city.

Song: Pandit, baad bade so jhootha

LOOK, THE WORLD HAS GONE MAD

Seekers, look, the world has gone mad
If you speak the truth, they beat you up
If you speak falsehoods, they believe you

Hindus shout, Raam is ours!
Muslims shout, Rahman!
They die fighting each other
Neither understands the essence

I've met many a pious man
Taking ritual morning baths
Ignorant of self, they worship stones
All their learning is humbug

They meditate with pomp and show
Hearts filled with arrogance
They worship trees or idols of stone
Lost in fasting and pilgrimage

They put on showy caps or beads
Adorn their skin with marks of faith
They sing songs or quote poetry
Devoid of any experience of self

They go around initiating others
Self-important, full of conceit
Such gurus and disciples both sink
Lamenting their folly at the end

I've seen so-called sages and saints
They quote the Qur'an and holy texts
Take on disciples, bow at graves
None of them came close to God

They mock me and laugh at me
And call themselves wise and sane
Kabir says, listen fellow seekers
Who among us is the mad one?

Song: Saadho dekho jag bauraana

YOU HAVE A STRANGE KIND OF GOD

You have a strange kind of God

The Mullah cries out in the mosque
Is your God hard of hearing?
If an ant wore an anklet
God would hear even that

The Pundit sits in rigid postures
Turning a long rosary
Within the heart, the dagger of deceit
Will you find God like this?

You build palaces, high and low
You dig a deep foundation
No desire to walk on the path
You'd rather stay and luxuriate

Bit by bit you amassed a fortune
Buried it deep in the earth
Take it away who wants!
Death awaits this scoundrel

Spurning the jewel you've been given
You busy yourself with trifles
Kabir says, listen fellow seekers
Hari is your own reflection.

Song: Na jaane tera saahib kaisa hai

You Don't Heed the Divine Music

The primordial drum beats
Throbbing softly, in your temple
You don't heed the divine music
So what if you hear all that's external?

Heroin, hemp, opium, dope
You consume spirits and alcohol
Never tasted the drink of love
So what if you're a wine-drinker?

You went to Varanasi or Dwarka
Roamed in all the pilgrim spots

Never loosened the knots of deceit
So what if you've been to holy places?

You pore over countless books
You preach endless sermons
Never entered your inner mansion
So what if you blabber forever?

The priest consults the holy book
Dispenses edicts and advice
Has no grasp of the living truth
So what if he set up as priest?

Yogis, sadhus, ascetics, monks
Dye their cloths in many colours
No inkling of that one colour
So what if your robe is ochre?

Temple, terrace, tent or garden
I'm ever present in all
Kabir speaks only this truth
The lord pulsates in every breath.

Song: Sunta nahin dhun ki khabar, anhad ka baaja baajta

YOU DON'T COLOUR YOUR HEART

You don't colour your heart, yogi
You only wear coloured clothes
You don't turn your mind, yogi
You turn only the rosary

You set up inside a temple
And sit in a stiff pose
You neglect the Absolute
And idolize a stone

You wear bulky earrings
And brandish dreadlocks
You've got a long beard
Now you look like a goat!

You trot off to the forest
And start a ritual fire
You smear yourself with ash
Now you look a perfect ass!

You shave off your hair
And dye your robes saffron
You try to kill desire
And become utterly impotent

Kabir says this,
Listen well seekers
You'll be nabbed by the neck
At the doorstep of Death.

Song: Mann na rangaaye, rangaaye jogi kapda

My Raam Rahim Karim Krishna

My Raam Rahim Karim Krishna
Allah, Raam are the same truth

Cease violence, the lord is one
There is none other

These guys have Qazis and Mullahs,
Sufis, prophets and Ramadan fasts,
Daily prayers to the west
Those guys have gods of the east,
Eleventh-day fasts and holy dips,
Temples, chants and bells

Muslims mosques, Hindus temples
The two have their Raam and Allah
Where there is no mosque, no temple
Who is the master there?

Hindus, Muslims both misguided
Rent apart and fragmented
Up and down, in all directions
There is only Raam, the Supreme One

Says Kabir, devotee, fakir
Walk your own path, brother
Hindus Muslims have the same maker
That truth is beyond conception.

Song: Hamaare Raam Rahim Karim Kesav Allah Raam sat soi

Folks, You're So Simple-Minded

Folks, you're so simple-minded
If Kabir were to get free

Simply by dying in Kashi
Then why all this bother about Raam?[9]

Now you're here, next you're there
This is all you get from life
Like water merges with water
So Kabir will mix with dust

Those really absorbed in Raam
They are not amazed by this
The guru's grace, truthful company
The weaver wins over the world

Die in Maghar, you'll never die
Die elsewhere, Raam will cry
You think dying in Maghar
will make you an ass?
Have you no
understanding of Raam?

Kabir says, listen good people
If you still don't get it
As Kashi by the river,
so arid Maghar
The two are identical once Raam
has occupied your heart.

Song: Loka mati ke bhora re

THE SECRET OF SONG IS UNSPEAKABLE

The secret of song is unspeakable
A rare one grasps it, O wanderer

Why do you sing, write, preach
What for this constant movement?
What use your prayers and rituals
Without contemplating the essence?

Why shave your head or sport dreadlocks
Or smear ash all over your skin?
Why this endless bowing to a stone
Or obsession with what you're eating?

He who sets up as sage without vision
Gripped by lures of mind and sense
Doesn't penetrate the heart of wisdom
His speech swells up with arrogance

Pathless, boundless, of an untold depth
Neither field nor seed remain
Absorbed in intense concentration
Wiping out all karmic stain

Those who feed only on the inner
Those who contemplate the core
Listen to what Kabir says, O Gorakh
They and their kin will reach that shore.

Song: Avadhu, bhajan bhed hai nyaara

THE TARGET IS BEYOND THE SKY

The target is beyond the sky

Sun on the right, moon on the left
It's hidden between the two

Body, the bow, attention, the string
Aim with the arrow of the Word

The arrow strikes, penetrates the body!
Such is the guru's commandment

The arrow strikes, no wounds on the body
Only one who is struck will know

Kabir says, listen seekers
Only one who knows will believe.

Song: Gagan ki ot nisaana hai

STICK TO YOUR PRACTICE

Remember Raam
And stick to your practice
Let the world brawl and fight

Black ink and a blank sheet
Lost in words
Let them read and write

The elephant proceeds at his own pace
Let the barking dogs
Bark and bay

This, that or the other goddess
Those who idolize
Let them bow and pray

Kabir says, listen seekers
Those who insist on hell
Let them go to hell.

Song: Tu to Raam sumar jag ladne de

MEDITATE, MY FRIEND

Dwell, dear friend
On Raam, Govind, Hari

Meditate, my friend
On Raam, Govind, Hari

It doesn't require
Austerities or long practice
Costs you nothing

Wealth and family
Bring pleasure
But also forgetfulness

Remember Raam's name
Death hangs like a sword
Over your head

Kabir says, one without
Raam on his lips
Bites the dust.

Song: Bhajo re bhaiya Raam Govind Hari

DEVOTION'S TOUGH, MY FRIEND![10]

Devotion's tough, my friend!
Love for the guru is hard
Without it acts have no grace
You swim to your apocalypse

Like the brainfever bird trills madly
For rain under an auspicious star
It prefers thirst to any other water
Even if it's breathing its last

Like the deer drawn to the Word
It comprehends the secret of sound
It gives up its life to hear the Word
Not a shred of fear to be found

Like two armies face each other
Only the brave take up this fight
Even if they get hacked to pieces
Never dream of resorting to flight

Like the widow abandons her home
Following her husband to the pyre
Gladly she surrenders her life
No fear when she sees the fire

Shedding all personal want
Sing of splendour fearlessly
If, says Kabir, such is your devotion
The guru will appear spontaneously.

Song: Guru se lagan kathin hai bhai

DARK RAIN CLOUDS HAVE GATHERED

In the sky, O practitioner
Dark rain clouds have gathered

The clouds come from the east
Bringing a soft rain
Wake up, seeker, prepare your field
The water's flowing away

Yoke the twin bulls
Of being rapt and mindful
Cultivate a constant field
Weed out the grass of doubt
Sow the seed of Sound

Attentive, adept, guard your crop
Don't let deer graze your field

Harvest, grind, bring home the yield
This is the art of farming

Five women friends cook the meal
One more able than the other
They serve two equal portions
Contemplatives and sages eat

Kabir says, listen fellow seekers
This song describes liberation
One who can fathom its depths
Call that one a learned person.

Song: Avadhu, gagan ghata gehraani

THE DRINK OF RAAM

The drink of Raam
Is incredibly sweet, O yogi
One who drinks it never dies

I burnt down my house, yogi
I took up the flaming torch
If you can burn your house, yogi
Then join me on this walk

Raze the house and a house arises, yogi
Protect it and it's gone!
I witnessed a miracle, yogi
A dead man was eating time

A fire blazes ahead, yogi
In its wake, greenery thrives
I'm devoted to that tree, yogi
Cut the root and the fruit revives

Dhruv drank it, Prahlad drank it, yogi
Peepa and Ravidas drank it in
Kabir delights in this nectar, yogi
Eager to drink it again and again.

Song: Raam ras meetho ghano jogiya ji

WHY WANDER ALL OVER?

Your Raam is in your heart
Why wander all over?

Such rare gems hidden in the body
Who but a jeweller can know their worth?

Such pure ghee hidden in the milk
Will butter emerge without churning?

Such sweet nectar hidden in sugarcane
Can juice be got without grinding?

Such bright flames hidden in firewood
Will fire ignite without friction?

Such big bolts studded on the heart
Who but the guru can open these locks?

Kabir says, listen seekers
You can't find Raam without stillness

Your Raam is in your heart
Why wander all over?

Song: Thaaro Raam hirday mein, baahar kyon bhatke?

TIME IS SLIPPING AWAY

Time is slipping away, my friend
Meditate, time is passing by
Take the path of Raam's name
Drop your foolish pride

O wise one, I was the first to be born
Then my elder brother
With great pomp, my father was born
In the end my mother

O wise one, first the yogurt was set
Then the cow got milked
The calf was still in the womb
When the cowgirl sold the butter

The ant goes to meet her husband
Nine bags of kohl, her dowry
She carries an elephant in one hand
A camel in the other

The unborn child could speak
The newborn child says nothing
Says Kabir, listen seekers
Fools can't figure it out.

Song: Ber chalya mera bhai

STRANGE ARE THE WAYS OF NATURE

O Seeker,
Strange are the ways of nature
Paupers are transformed into kings
And emperors into beggars

Clove trees don't bear fruit
Sandalwood doesn't flower
A fish prowls the forest like a hunter
A lion swims at sea

A dry castor-oil plant
Turns to fragrant sandalwood
In all parts of all universes
A blind man witnesses the spectacle

A lame man scales the highest peaks
And roams free in the three worlds
A dumb man unveils the utmost wisdom
And speaks in an ancient idiom

A packed-up sky is plunged to the depths
The great serpent rules over heaven

Kabir says, Raam is King
Whatever he does is becoming.

Song: Avadhu, kudrat ki gat nyaari

HERMIT, RIDDLE ME THIS WISDOM

O hermit, riddle me this wisdom
Climb a boat, you drown midstream
With no support, you cross over

Walk on no path, you reach the city
Walk on the road, you're ambushed
The same rope binds everybody
Who is tied, who is free?

Stay at home, you get drenched
Step outside, you're dry
Fully dead, you're ever happy
Escape death, you're forlorn

No eyes, but you see everything
Open eyes, and you're blind
Kabir says, did you understand anything?
I've seen the world is a scam.

Song: Avadhu, aisa gyaan vichaar

I SAW A WONDROUS SIGHT

Friend, I saw a wondrous sight
A lion was shepherding cows

First the child
Then the mother was born
The guru bowed down
To the disciple

Fish climbed trees
To lay their eggs
The cock caught the cat
And ate it up

The sack came home
With the bull on its back
The cat made off
With the dog in its mouth

Branches put below
Roots placed on top
Many kinds of flowers
Grow on the roots

Kabir says one
Who can understand this
Will glimpse the secret
Of all three worlds.

Song: Ek achambha dekha re bhai

THE WAVES OF THE OCEAN

The waves of the ocean
Are still the ocean

Is there a distinction
Between the wave and the ocean?

Rising, it's water
Falling, it's water
Then how is it so
That you call them two?

You give it a different name
And call it a wave
If you call it a wave
Does it stop being water?

The world full of names
Is still Universal Oneness
Kabir says
Look with the eyes of wisdom.

Song: Dariyaav ka lahar dariyaav hai ji

TELL ME THE SECRET OF THIS

O yogi, tell me the secret of this
Let all your actions be good
In tree, flower and all creation
Wherever I look, there's you, just you

As an ant, you become minuscule
As an elephant, you grow huge
You're the elephant's keeper too
Driving him on, you, just you

Among thieves, you act as a thief
Among rogues, you're one too
You loot and you run away
The cop who nabs you is also you

In the giver, you are the giver
You are one with the beggar too
You get hard up and beg for alms
The one who provides is also you

One in both man and woman
Why do we insist on two?
As a child, you begin to cry
The one who pacifies you is also you

On land, in water, in every creature
Wherever I look, I see you, just you
Kabir says, listen fellow seekers
I found the guru, true as true.

Song: Jahaan dekhun vahaan tu ka tu

THAT BIRD SINGS IN EVERY BEING

That bird sings
In every being

Itself the balance
Itself the weights
Itself the one who
Holds the scales

Itself the gardener
Itself the garden
Itself the one who
Plucks fresh flowers

In each one
It's become that one
In mind and matter
In both it pulsates

Kabir says
Listen those who seek
It opens the lock
On your heart.

Song: Ghat ghat mein panchhi bolta

MY HEART'S BECOME A DANCER

My heart's become a dancer
It's on its feet
Night and day, day and night
The drums of wisdom beat
Everyone's tuned in
To the Word's heartbeat

Planets and stars are swinging
Mountain, ocean, earth, all singing
All humans dance
Whether laughing or weeping
There is joy in the city of death

Proud of name and status
You climb a pedestal
Feeling superior to others
With a thousand graces
My heart dances
Wooing the creator

Thrown into the world-ocean
Swim with the skill of stillness
Kabir says, listen seeker
Become a real disciple.

Song: Naachu re mero mann nat hoy

Fakiri

My mind is absorbed in fakiri
My heart rejoices in simplicity

The joy I found in Raam remembrance
Cannot be had in mere affluence

A bowl and a staff are all I carry
Yet my kingdom stretches as far as I see

Praise or abuse, listen to it all
Yet abide in austerity

My dwelling in the city of love
Became beautiful with humility

Your body will bite the dust one day
Why strut about, so smug, so vain?

Kabir says, listen fellow seekers
The Lord is found in equanimity.

Song: Mann laago mero yaar fakiri mein

MY HEART'S FULL OF JOY

My heart's full of joy
What's left to say
My mind's intoxicated
Nothing more to say

You found a jewel,
Put it in your pocket
Why keep taking it
Out for display?

Feeling inadequate,
You climbed the scale
You're full now
What's there to weigh?

Awareness, the bartender
Drank her own wine
The endless intoxication
Is making her sway

The swan swims and sports
In the great mountain lake

In ponds and puddles
Why do you stay?

Your master hides
Within your self
Why keep turning
Out your gaze?

Kabir says,
Listen seekers
I found the Lord
In a piece of grain.

Song: Mann mast hua phir kya bole?

THE MIND BECAME RAPT

The mind became rapt
On hearing that sound

Full absorption
At the guru's feet
Oh friend, at last,
All sorrow was dissolved

A thread was strung
On the spine of the Word
The swan climbed on
And flew into freedom

On the peak of emptiness
Adornments glimmer

Nectar showers
Love seeps in

Kabir says, listen seekers
Drink after drink
Induced in me
Ecstasy.

Song: Dhun sun ke manva magan hua ji

MY GIRLHOOD HOME

I have no joy
In my parents' home
I can't stay any more
In my girlhood home

The beloved's city
Is of breathtaking beauty
Where no one enters nor leaves
No sun, no moon
No wind, no water
Who can take my message there?
Who will tell him of my pain?

I can't see the way ahead
To turn back would be folly
How can I reach
The beloved's house, oh friend?
The fever of longing burns me
Sensory delights make me
Dance to their tune

Who can you call your own
Except the true guru
Who else can show the way?
Kabir says, listen seekers
The beloved doesn't come in a dream
To douse the heart's flames.

Song: Naiharva hamka na bhaavai

My Heart Aches

My heart aches
Without my beloved

My heart's in torment
Bereft of my beloved

Fretful days, sleepless nights
Tossing and turning the dawn arrives

Mind and body in a whirl
A tainted life on a barren bed

Weary eyes strain to look
The cruel beloved does not appear

Kabir says, listen seekers
O master, relieve me of this sorrow.

Song: Tadpe bin baalam mora jiya

This Alien Country

It's not for me
This alien country

Can't stay any more
In this barren land

This world is a ball of paper
A splash of water, and it crumbles

This world is a thorny garden
It ensnares and entangles

This world is dry tinder
Just one spark, and it burns

Kabir says, listen seekers
The guru's wisdom is my true home.

Song: Rehna nahin des veeraana hai

No One Is Yours

No one is yours
Understand, oh heart

Your wealth and gold
Your precious riches
A passing dream

We come naked
And go naked
No covering remains

From between the brows
Life escapes
A shroud covers the face

Four pall-bearers
Haul the bed
Into a wasteland

A bed of wood
Laid out in the wild
You burn to dust

Kabir says
Listen seekers
That is our real home.

Song: Koi nahin apna, samajh mana

CITY OF THE DEAD

Brothers, look,
A city of the dead

Dying gurus, dying prophets
Highly revered yogis dying
Dying kings, dying subjects
Doctors and the diseased, dying

Dying suns, dying moons
Earth and sky are dying too
Marked by death, the lord of the world
What hope for them or us?

The nine Naths, the ten avatars
Eighty-eight thousand saints, all perish
Thirty-three crore gods all doomed
Trapped by the noose of Death

The nameless Name remains forever
There is none other
Kabir says, listen seekers
Don't just drift through life and die.

Song: Saadho ye murdon ka gaon

THE SWAN WILL FLY AWAY ALONE

The swan will fly away alone
This world, a picture gallery
A pageant of events

Like the leaf breaks away from the tree
Never to unite again
Who knows where it will land
Blown by a gust of wind

When at last this life is spent
Then this servitude comes to an end

Death's minions are awfully potent
The final tussle is with Death

Humble Kabir sings of Hari's glory
He delights in Hari's immensity
The guru's actions are his harvest
The disciple must look to his own

The swan will fly away alone.

Song: Ud jaayega hans akela

OH MIND, YOU STRUT ABOUT

Oh mind, you strut about
Puffed up, full of yourself
What in the world is yours?

Mother says, 'my son'
Sister says, 'my brother'
Brother calls you his right arm
Wife proclaims, 'my husband'

Your mother weeps inconsolably
Your brother cannot bear the loss
The wife tears her hair out
But the swan goes alone

Your mother mourns you all her life
Sister grieves for a while after
Wife weeps for the allotted period
Then she looks out for another

Your body's wrapped up in a shroud
Mounted on a wooden chariot
Set aflame on every corner
Blazing like a bonfire

Bones burn like firewood
Hair burns like grass
This golden body utterly charred
No one comes near any more

The wife starts to search again
She's out and about already
Kabir says, listen fellow seekers
Release your hunger for the world.

Song: Mann phoola phoola phire

DRIVE THIS CART SLOWLY

Drive this cart slowly
Oh my Raam of the cart
Move this cart gently
Oh, master of this cart

My cart is colourful, beautiful
The wheels are red and rosy
A sassy young girl drives it on
Raam is the passenger

The cart gets stuck in the mud
The destination's still far away

Upright ones make it there
Evildoers are crushed

Healers summoned from every land
Came with their herbs and cures
None of it was useful to you
When you lost the connection with Raam

Four people gather together
Place you on a wooden bier
Haul you to the funeral grounds
Up you go in flames like Holi

The wife weeps in great distress
Our couple has been torn apart
Kabir says, listen seekers
One who joins, tears asunder.

Song: Zara halke gaadi haanko, mere Raam gaadi vaale

This Body Is Like a String

Seekers, this body is like the string
Of a musical instrument

Twist the peg,
Tune the string
The spirit bursts into song

The string snaps,
The peg disintegrates
Nothing remains but dust

Don't be proud of this body
The swan of this lute
Will fly away

Kabir says, listen seekers
The warrior's way
Is formidable.

Song: Saadho yeh tan thaat tambure ka

THE GURU GIVES THE ETERNAL NAME

The guru gives the eternal Name
There's no one like the guru
Storerooms spilling over with grace
A place of no lack

Such a gift as the Name
Is not for an unmindful person
Like an owl knows only star-light
It knows nothing of the sun

It doesn't deplete by spending
It isn't gutted by burning
Futile your study of holy texts
Only the guru can grant the Name

The sun bursts over earth and sea
Moon and stars are swept away
So, all chants, yoga, austerities
Are effaced in front of the Name

The desiring mind loses awareness
Meditate on the true Name
The divine is in yourself, Kabir
Make this inner pilgrimage.

Song: Guruji ne diyo amar naam

I'M A BIRD FROM ANOTHER LAND

I'm a bird from another land
Not of this country
People here live in forgetfulness
Folly, regret, at every step

Talk without tongue, walk without feet
Flight without wings
My attention free of all illusions
I glide in boundless freedom

To sit in the shade feels hot
Being in the sun feels cool
My guru's beyond sun and shade
I soak in that truth

Firm in resolve at all hours
A true master never wavers
Mind and breath don't reach there
That land to which I belong

My lord is one without a form
He takes on a thousand names

Kabir says, meet with that one
Overcome decay and death.

Song: Ham pardesi panchhi baba, ani des ra naahin

FOR AGES I'VE BEEN A YOGI

Listen, O ascetic
For ages I've been a yogi
He neither comes nor goes
One who has consumed
The immutable Word

In every place, a gathering
My gathering
In every place, a carnival
I'm in all, all are in me
I'm many and alone

I'm the meditator
I, the meditation
I stay silent and I speak
Seeing through form,
Great form, no form
I'm at play within myself

Listen to what Kabir says, O seekers
Not a single desire left
In my small hut, I stay

I sway, I play
Naturally, spontaneously,
Free.

> Song: Avadhoota, yugan yugan ham yogi

THAT HOUSE IS UTTERLY DIFFERENT

That house is utterly different, friend
Where that perfect consciousness dwells

No joy or grief, no truth or lies
No good or evil there
No sun or moon, no day or night
Illumination without sight

No erudition, meditation or mantra
No scripture or holy book
Action, possessions, mores, convention
In that place, all forgotten

No earth or sky, no inside-outside
No micro- or macro-cosm
No five elements, no three forces
No poetic compositions

No root, no bud, no vine, no seed
Fruit shines forth without a tree
No inhale-exhale, up- or down-energy
No one to watch the breath carefully

Neither form nor formlessness
Nothing called gross or subtle
Neither secret nor eternal
These are fundamental errors

Where that consciousness is,
there is nothing else
Kabir says I've experienced this
One who can follow these signs
Will attain an unchained mind.

Song: Sakhi va ghar sabse nyaara

I KNOW THE GREAT CROOK MAYA

I know the great crook Maya
She controls the three forces
And casts her net wide
Talking a sweet tongue

In Vishnu's home, she's lodged as Lakshmi
In Shiva's domain, Parvati
In the priest's mind, she settles as an idol
In the holy river, she's seen as water

For the yogi, she comes as a yogini
For the king, she acts like his queen
For someone, she shines like a diamond
For another, a few coins are everything

For a devotee, it's his devotion
For Bramha, the act of creation
Kabir says, listen seekers
This fable is unfathomable.

Song: Maya maha thagini ham jaani

FEARLESSLY, I'LL SING

Fearlessly, I'll sing
The praises of the formless
Reality beyond particularity

Tightening the root centre
I'll set a firm foundation
Reverse the breath, make it climb upwards

Stilling the mind
And its attachments
I'll unite the five elements

Left, right and centre
Three energy streams
I'll bathe at their confluence

I'll tame the five
And twenty-five to my will
I'll string them on one thread

On the peak of emptiness
The throb of eternal sound
I'll sing all possible melodies

Kabir says, listen seekers
I will blazon forth
The mark of victory.

Song: Nirbhay nirgun gun re gaaunga

A Rare and Wise Guru Listens

A rare and wise guru listens
A sound in the sky, so subtle

It came from primal drop and sound
Took shape in these waters
It fully informs each body
Unspeaking unseen awareness

You were sent with an agreement
Designed to quench your thirst
Spurning nectar, you drink poison
Tangled in a twisted web

A sky seen without an earth
Water gathers without a lake
The sky-dome fills up with light
The guru speaks words of wisdom

A cow gave milk in the sky
The yogurt was set on earth
True seekers took home the butter
The rest got only buttermilk

Drums of in- and out-breath beat
Between the brows, a sparkling site
I've seen the channels, mid, left and right
And planted my flag in the void

Perceive it whole, in every moment
It's the mark of deathlessness
Kabir says, listen fellow seekers
I sing this transcendent truth.

Song: Koi sunta hai guru gyaani

O RAAM, UNTANGLE THIS KNOT

O Raam, untangle this knot
If you really care about your folk

Is Bramha bigger
Or where he came from?
Are the Vedas bigger
Or their creators?

Is the mind bigger
Or the mind's belief?
Is Raam bigger
Or the knower of Raam?

Kabir says,
At my wit's end, I wonder
Are holy spots bigger
Or the pilgrim travellers?

Song: Jhagda ek navero Raam

Select Dohas of Kabir

Kabir stands in the marketplace
Flaming torch in hand
If you can burn your house down
Come, walk with me!

Kabir stands in the marketplace
Wishing everyone well
No special friendship
Nor any ill-will.

Kabir, when you were born
The world rejoiced and you wept
Live so, that when you go
You rejoice and the world weeps.

Act today, not tomorrow
Act now, not today
Apocalypse comes in a flash!
Too much will be left undone.

Seeing the millstones grind
Kabir breaks into lament
Crushed between the two slabs
No one is spared.

The clay says to the potter
You may pound me today
But a day is bound to come
When you will be pounded by me.

The wooden rosary wonders
Why turn me round and round?
Turn the beads of your heart instead
You'll connect instantly.

Speak in such a tongue
That you go beyond self-obsession
Words that refresh others
As well as refreshing yourself.

Never touched ink or paper
Never held a pen in hand
The wisdom of all four ages
Kabir proclaimed with his tongue.

Reading book after book, they died
Not one of them became wise
Read the four letters of love
That's how you become wise.

Reading endlessly, you've become a stone
Writing endlessly, you've become a brick

Kabir says, not one drop of love
Has touched your skin.

It's not a matter of reading and writing
It's a matter of experience
When the bride and groom meet in union
The wedding party is of no significance.

Don't ask about a seeker's caste
Ask about his wisdom
Value the sword within
Not the outer sheath.

Both Guru and Govind stand before me
Whose feet should I touch first?
I surrender to the Guru
Who showed me the path to Govind.

When I was, Hari wasn't
Now Hari is, I am not
The path of love is extremely narrow
Two cannot fit in it.

I set out in search of evil
I found no one bad
When I looked within myself
No one worse than I.

Kabir, your hut is next to
Cut-throats and butchers
As they sow, so shall they reap
Why lose your sleep?

Why act and be afraid?
Why regret, having acted?
If you plant a thorny tree
Why expect to reap mangoes?

Kabir, cheat yourself
But never cheat another
Cheating yourself brings happiness
Cheating others brings sorrow.

Desires gone, and worries with them!
The mind is now carefree
She who longs for nothing
Is the true emperor of the world.

Slowly, oh heart, slowly
Everything happens slowly
The gardener may pour endless water
But the fruit appears only in season.

Aim for the one, you'll attain all
Aim for all, you'll lose the one
When the gardener waters the root
There are fruits and flowers aplenty.

Oh lord, give as much
As is sufficient for the family
That there be enough for me to eat
As well as for the monk's begging bowl.

Kabir says to Kamaal,
Keep two things in your heart

Always remember the creator
And give food to the hungry.

Why all this chant of 'Kabir', 'Kabir'?
Search within your own self
When you look into your own body
You will be Kabir yourself.

Kabir, the heart has become pure
Like the waters of the Ganga
Now Hari comes running after me
Shouting, 'Kabir, Kabir!'

Like the sesame seed contains oil
Like the flintstone contains fire
Your master is within you
Wake up, if you can!

Kabir says, the well is one
Water-bearers many
Each one has a different vessel
But they all contain the same water.

The drop is in the ocean
Everyone knows this
That the ocean is in a drop
A rare one knows this.

Oh lord, your divinity
Is contained in every body
Like redness in a henna leaf
Stays hidden, unseen.

My beloved's coloured in red
Now wherever I look, I see red
I set out in search of red
I became red myself.

Everyone hankers for the ruby
Though they have it in their pockets!
You never looked at what you have
And so you feel like a pauper.

Body the pot, mind the churning-stick
Awareness, the one who churns
Kabir ate up all the butter
The world's content with buttermilk.

So what if you've reached high up
Like the date-palm tree
You give no shade to travellers
And your fruit is far away.

Greatness doesn't sing its own praises
A great person doesn't brag
A diamond doesn't proclaim loudly
I'm worth a million bucks.

Water doesn't stay in high places
It runs to lower ground
Those who try to be high and mighty
They die of thirst.

What's all this talk of 'low caste'
Gopal dwells within my heart
Kabir has embraced his Raam
He's out of all this mess.

The whole world is lost
In arrogance about caste
Without experience of the truth
All four castes are 'low'.

You didn't meditate on Raam
You didn't stay close to Hari
What's the point of regret now
When birds have eaten your crop?

Hindus die muttering Raam
Muslims die chanting Khuda
Kabir says that one really lives
Who never enters into duality.

If by worshipping a stone you could find God
I would worship a big mountain!
A better use of stone is the grinding mill
It provides flour for the whole world.

Scrambling some bricks together
You built a great mosque
The mullah climbs to the roof and shouts
Has God gone deaf?

What harm did your hair do to you
Why do you keep shaving your head?
Why not shave your mind instead
Which is full of hankering?

O yogi, you have no idea of the path
So what if you coloured your cloth?
The heresy of your heart is intact, O qazi
So what if you loudly avow your faith?

Kabir has pointed out
This absurdity a thousand times
You want to be a sheep
And yet arrive at liberation.

Kabir's house is on the mountain-top
And the path up is slippery
Even an ant loses its footing there
Why load your bullock-cart, O pundit?

Speakers, scholars, priests and poets
Roam the world in countless numbers
But one who has tasted truth
That is a rare seeker.

Pundit, throw your books into water
Qazi, let go of your Quran
Tell me of that date, that time
When there was neither earth nor sky.

The pundit and the torch-bearer
Neither really understands

They show the light to others
But themselves remain in darkness.

Reading endless books
The world lies tired and flat
If you haven't felt the pain of love
How can you utter a single true word?

Everyone says 'I'm moved', 'I'm struck'
But to be struck is a terrible thing
You can truly say you're struck
If you've been cut through and through.

We all came from one country
And landed in one place
A wall of ignorance within
Split us into a dozen paths.

Kabir, the wares were spread
And the deal was done
You took the fake gems with glee
Couldn't pick out the real ones.

Kabir, the dark age is here
No saint is respected
Falsehood, cunning, greed
These are worshipped.

Kabir, you're better off losing
Let the world win its races
The winner is carried off by death
The loser lands at Hari's doorstep.

Worry ate up everyone
Worry is everyone's real guru
One who swallows worry down
That one is a real fakir.

Keep a critic close
Shelter him in your house
Without soap or water
He cleanses your insides.

There's a mirror in your heart
But your face is not visible
You can only see your true face
When your heart is free of duality.

Don't follow the mind's ways
The mind leads you here and there
Destroy the mind in such a way
That it shatters to pieces.

The mind's greedy, the mind's avaricious
The mind's unsteady, the mind's a thief!
Don't follow the mind's ways
It changes every moment.

Don't follow the mind's ways
The mind has twists and turns
One who can rein the mind
That seeker's a rare one.

Lose to the mind and you lose
Win over the mind and you win

This very mind can lead to Raam
This very mind can lead to ruin.

Minds have died, affections died
Body after body has suffered death
Hope and desire have still not died
So states Kabir.

The mind made you scamper
You ran as far as the mind could fare
Tired of its flight the mind grew still
And the object was right there.

The mind has as many turns
As there are waves in the ocean
The pearl forms naturally, spontaneously
When the mind is stilled.

Awareness got entangled in things
This caused an alienation
Bridle the attention and make it still
Then the Lord is always with you.

Awareness divorced from the Word is blind
Where can it come to rest?
It can't find the gateway to the Word
Keeps wandering here and there.

All renounce grosser illusions
No one gives up the subtle ones
The subtle delusion devours
Gurus, prophets and holy men.

For one who gives up subtle attachments
The gross fall off by themselves
Kabir says for such a seeker
All sorrows come to an end.

Remember the Name in each breath
Don't let a single breath go in vain
Who knows if in the next moment
Another breath will come again?

Make a practice of the Name
Chant the chantless chant
Concentrate on the ultimate essence
Then you are that.

String 'I am that' into the breath
Tie your attention to the most high
Fasten the divine knot in your heart
This is how to turn the rosary.

The rosary is of the breath
Only a true seeker turns it
One who stops endless wandering
And snaps the chain of birth and death.

Sleep within waking
Attachment within sleep
One makes a home in the forest
Another stays at home and is detached.

I'm looking for such a seeker
Who doesn't cause hurt

Doesn't damage leaves or flowers
Yet stays in the garden.

Long have you wandered, Kabir
Let the mind cease its quests
You've been searching for ages
In every particle, Raam rests.

Kabir, stay away from erudition
Throw all the books away!
Forget the letters of the alphabet
Focus your mind on 'Ra' and 'ma'.

Melody is the form of Raam
The melody contains Raam
Listen with great attention
It's not visible to the eyes.

All forests became sacred
And all mountains holy
All rivers became like the Ganga
When I found the Raam within.

Raam chants in my every vein
And echoes in every pore
The vibration arises spontaneously
This is the essence of meditation.

I don't turn the rosary beads
I don't chant the name of Raam
Now Raam chants my name
And I am at ease!

Raam's name flows in abundance
Gather it with both hands, if you can
Or in the end you'll repent
When life ebbs out of you.

I set up the beam of Raam's name
And strung the thread of the sun
Follow the rise and fall of breath
This is the path to liberation.

A diamond lies in the market street
People step over it heedlessly
When a true jeweller passes by
He will pick it up immediately.

Kabir, our true earnings
Are never really lost
You may wander the seven seas
They still await you at the end.

Kabir, this boat is wobbly
And the boatmen are inept
They got across who were light
The heavy ones drowned.

If all this 'me' and 'mine' ended
Then there would be space
When the mind becomes still
It finds its resting-place.

As long as we chant, I, I, I
All our acts are haphazard and awry

When we destroy the obsession with I
Hari himself makes our actions worthwhile.

Nothing in me is mine
Whatever's there is yours
I give back to you what is yours
What can I say is 'mine'?

Whatever was done was done by you
This mortal could do nothing
Even if I say I did something
You were in me doing it.

Words as sweet as sugar
Actions like a lump of poison
When words and actions harmonize
Poison turns into nectar.

Everyone speaks of 'sahaj', of simplicity
No one understands its meaning
She who attains Hari with simplicity
Call her the 'sahaj' one.

Is there a saint of spontaneous bliss
I'll trade him all my spiritual practices
To fulfil with one drop of Raam-nectar
Like the bartender fills a glass of wine.

The musk lies in its own sac
Yet the deer hunts for it in the forest
So Raam resides in every body
Fools don't get this.

Rubies are not found in sackfuls
Swans don't move in flocks
Lions are not found in herds
And a true seeker walks alone.

The pond is small, swarming with storks
Now is your opportunity, O swan!
Don't mess around in this puddle
You're a native of the ocean, O swan!

One who sought, attained
Entering into deep waters
I, a fool, feared drowning
And stayed put at the shore.

In the centre of the sky-circle
Radiance shimmers
One without a guide can't make it there
Only a true warrior may enter.

Where's the object, where the search?
And how will you attain it?
You'll find the object right here
If you have an insider to guide you.

If the whole earth became paper
And all the trees became pens
And all the seas became ink
The guru would still be indescribable.

This body is like poison ivy
The guru, a pool of nectar

Guru, in exchange for your head?
It's a good bargain!

If I say 'yes', it isn't so
But I also cannot say 'no'
My true guru is to be found
In the space between 'yes' and 'no'.

My guru's in the sky
The disciple is in awareness
Attention and Sound thus meet
Never to separate again.

The guru is the potter, disciple the pot
He shapes the pot and irons out flaws
The hand inside gives support
The hand outside beats into shape.

The guru's out on a hunt
Red bow and arrow in hand
The fools escape unhurt
A real seeker is struck down!

Some strike with guns and arrows
Your body is covered with wounds
My true guru strikes with the Word
The world is turned upside down.

My true guru is a trader
His business is widespread
Without a measure or scales
He weighs up the whole world.

Two birds perch on a branch
The guru and the disciple
The disciple eats of the fruit
The guru is always at play.

All these are gurus of limitations
Not gurus of the unbound
In the house of experience
The unbounded arises spontaneously.

Gurus with big beards are bound
A guru beyond bounds is scarce
Find such a boundless guru
To arrive at your true abode.

Kabir says, only he is truly wise
Who knows the pain of another
He who knows not another's pain
Is directionless, a heretic.

Kabir's words are strange and absurd
You can't get them in a jiffy
Those who get them in a jiffy
Their troubles are over in a jiffy.

The earth turned into a piece of bread
The crow is flying away with it
Go ask your guru
Now where is he going to sit and eat it.

As long as the lion rules the jungle
The jungle cannot flourish or prosper

When the jackal devours the lion instead
The whole forest blossoms and thrives.

If you call me a Hindu, I'm not
But I'm not a Muslim either
The essence is in both
And I play in both!

Raam and Rahim are one
Don't think of them as two
There is a veil of delusion within
Which makes them appear two.

Raam and Rahim are one
Mecca and Varanasi are the same
One grain, many dishes
Kabir watches in wonder.

Mecca is Varanasi again
And Raam has become Rahim
The coarse grain has been ground fine
Kabir eats with relish.

There is one Raam, who was son of Dashrath
The second Raam is in every body
The third is in every inch of space
And the fourth is beyond even these.

Chanting your name, I passed into you
No 'me' remained in my 'I'
The cycle of becoming was sacrificed
Now wherever I look, I see you.

My beloved resides in every body
There is no bed that's empty
I bow down to each body
In whom the beloved manifests.

This is the house of love
Not your favourite aunt's house!
Cut off your head, put it on the floor
Then you may enter the house.

The drink of love is for one
Who can lay down her head
One full of greed can't give up her head
Though she may chant the name of love.

Either keep your precious pride
Or taste the drink of love
Two swords in a single sheath?
No one heard of such a thing.

Everyone talks about love
No one knows what love is
Unwavering love, which dwells within
That is called love.

Those in whom there is no love
They are like cremation grounds
Like the bellows of an ironsmith
They breathe without life.

Love doesn't grow in gardens
Love is not sold in markets

A person who has no love
Is dragged to death in chains.

The gait of a wounded one
Is different from that of others
When struck by the arrow of love
You find your true abode.

Love will not be hidden
In one in whom it appears
She may utter no words
But her tears will betray her.

The water-lily nestles in water
While the moon dwells in the sky
Whoever lives in another's heart
They are always together.

I would write letters to my love
If he lived far away
But what message can I send to one
Who is in my body, mind and eyes?

Come into my eyes, my love
I'll shut my eyes and hold you close
I won't look at anyone else
Nor let you look elsewhere.

Make your eyes a room
Make your pupils the bed
Make your eyelids the curtains
Make love to your beloved here.

Eyes full of love
This is the cause of grief
In love with the Name
The whole night spent in tears.

Eyes full of love
These tears flow night and day
Like the brainfever bird cries out
Constantly for its beloved.

Eat my whole body, crow
Pick all the flesh when I die
But spare these two little eyes
I still hope to glimpse my beloved!

The beloved has come home
How may I welcome him?
I prepare a tray of pearls
And place my eyes on top.

If my beloved's a red rose
Then I'm his fragrance
If he's my beating heart
Then I'm his breath.

I cry out beloved, beloved
The beloved is the root of being!
I've painted him into my bangles
Now I glance at him every moment.

Beloved, you and I are one
Why do we appear as two?

Balance one heart with another
They'll never appear as two.

Untellable is the tale of love
Beyond words
Like a dumb man eating sweets
Smiles silently.

This body's like a brittle clay pot
We carry it around everywhere
One blow and it shatters!
Nothing to hold on to any more.

Why do you strut about
Why do you parade yourself?
In a flash, apocalypse
Like a moth in a flame.

Kabir, why wander forgetfully
Why this deep sleep of unawareness?
Death stands by your bedside
Like a thief hides in the darkness.

All who have come will go
King, beggar or fakir
Some go seated on a throne
Some have to be dragged in chains.

Whatever arises has to set
Whatever flowers has to fade
Whatever is built has to fall
Whatever is born has to die.

That death which the world fears
Brings joy to my heart!
When will I die, when embrace
The bliss of wholeness?

The world dies death after death
No one knows the art of dying
Learn to die in such a way
That you never have to die again.

Kabir, many are those who visit
The winemaker's distillery
Only those who pay with heads may drink
This drink is not for others.

Tall tree, sky fruit
A rare bird eats
Only that one can reach it
Who dies while still alive.

I'm a pearl-diver of the ocean
Plunging into the deep
I bring back fistfuls of wisdom
Countless shining pearls.

From where does the Word arise?
Tell me, where does it go?
It has no hands or feet
Can one catch it or no?

From the navel-lotus it rises
Into emptiness it goes

It has no hands or feet
Awareness can catch its flow.

Body still, mind still, speech stilled as well
Attention and absorption still
Kabir says such a moment
Is beyond conception!

Remembering the Name, the mind was stilled
With words of wisdom, it became absorbed
Awareness and Word united
The fish dissolved into water.

Thinner than water
Subtler than smoke
Faster than wind
Kabir made friends with it.

A path walked without feet
A country without habitation
Consciousness without a body
Follow these signs, says Kabir.

Where no ant can climb
No space for even a grain
No mind or breath exist
Kabir is absorbed there.

Everyone fills water from the river
No one fills it from the no-river
Kabir's river is the no-river
That water truly purifies you.

Soul, my caste
Breath, my name
The invisible, my deity
The sky, my hometown.

Don't go to outer gardens
There are gardens within your body
Perched on the eight lotuses
You can see the multitude of forms.

First and foremost, Allah's radiance
All humans come from God
The same light created the whole world
Who is 'good' and who is 'bad'?

I merged with that one
Became one with everything
All are mine, I belong to all
There is no other.

You rule over everything
There is no one who rules you
You are formless, fearless
You inhabit all there is.

Settled within limits, they discourse
With no inkling of the limitless
When you glimpse the limitless
No more need for words.

I said all I had to
Now nothing more to say
One stayed, no other remained
Like a wave merges in the ocean.

Original Texts

Songs

Haman hain ishq mastaana,
haman ko hoshiyaari kya?
Rahein aazaad ya jag mein,
haman duniya se yaari kya?

Jo bichhude hain piyaare se,
bhatakte dar-badar phirte
Hamaara yaar hai ham mein,
haman ko intezaari kya?

Na pal bichhude piya ham se,
na ham bichhude piyaare se
Unhi se neh laagi hai,
haman ko bekaraari kya?

Khalak sab naam ko apne,
bahut kar sir patakta hai

Haman guru naam saacha hai,
haman ko naamdaari kya?

Kabira ishq ka maata,
dui ko door kar dil se
Jo chalna raah naazuk hai,
haman sir bojh bhaari kya?

∼

Jo khudaay masjid basat hai,
aur muluk kehi kera?
Teerath moorat Raam nivaasi,
dui mein kinahu na hera

Poorab disa Hari ko baasa,
pachhim Allah mukaama
Dil mein khoj dil hi mein khojo,
ihai Karima Raama

Ved kitaib kaha kin jhootha,
jhootha jo na vichaare
Sab ghat ek-ek kai lekhe,
bhay dooja ke maare

Jete aurat mard upaani,
so sab roop tumhaara
Kabir pongra Allah-Raam ka,
so guru-peer hamaara

∼

Moko kahaan dhoondhe bande,
main to tere paas mein

Na teerath mein, na moorat mein,
na ekaant nivaas mein
Na mandir mein, na masjid mein,
na Kaabe Kailash mein

Na main jap mein, na main tap mein,
na varat upaas mein
Na main kirya-karam mein rehta,
nahin yog sanyaas mein

Na main pind mein, na main praan mein,
na bramhand aakaash mein
Na main tirkuti bhanvar gufa mein,
sabhi svaans ki svaans mein

Khoji hoye turat mil jaaun,
ik pal ki talaash mein
Kahe Kabir suno bhai saadho,
main to hoon vishwaas mein

≈

Jheeni jheeni beeni chadariya
Raam ras ki beeni chadariya

Kaahe ke taana kaahe ke bharni,
kaun taar se beeni chadariya?
Ingla pingla taana bharni,
sukhman taar se beeni chadariya

Aath kamal dal charkha dole,
paanch tatva gun teeni chadariya
Saain ko bunat maas das laage,
thok thok ke beeni chadariya

So chaadar sur nar muni odhi,
odh ke maili keeni chadariya
Das Kabir ne jatan se odhi,
jyon ki tyon dhar deeni chadariya

~

Tanna bunna tajyo Kabir
Raam naam likh liyo shareer

Jab lag bharo nali ka beh
Tab lag toote Raam sneh

Thaadi rove Kabir ki maai
Ae ladka kivun jive Khudaai

Ochhi mat meri, jaat julaaha
Har ka naam liyo main laaha

Kahe Kabir sunahu ri maai
Pooranhaara tribhuvan raai

~

Saahib hai rangrez,
chunariya mori rang daali

Syaahi rang chhudaai ke,
diyo majeetha rang
Dhoye se chhoote nahin,
din din hot surang

Bhaav ke kund, neh ke jal mein,
prem rang dei bor
Deh dukh mail lutaai de,
khoob rangi jhakjhor

Saahib ne chunari rangi re,
preetam chatur sujaan
Sab kuchh un par vaar doon,
tan mann dhan aur praan

Kahe Kabir rangrez piyaare
mujh par hue dayaal
Seetal chunari odh ke,
bhayi hoon magan nihaal

~

Ghoonghat ke pat khol re,
toko piya milenge
Ghoonghat ke pat khol re

Ghat ghat mein vahi saain basat hai
Katuk vachan mat bol re

Dhan joban ka garab mat keeje
Jhootha panch rang chol re

Sunn mahal mein diya baari le
Aasha se mat dol re

Jog jugat se rang mahal mein
Piya paaye anmol re

Kahe Kabir anand bhayo hai
Baajat anhad dhol re

~

Santon bhai, aayi gyaan ki aandhi
Bhram ki taati sabai udaani,
maya rahe na baandhi

Duchite ki hai thooni giraani,
moh balinda toota
Trishna chhaani padi ghar upar,
kubudhi ka bhaanda phoota

Jog jugat kar santon baandhi,
nirchu chuvai na paani
Kood kapat kaaya ka niksya,
Hari ki gati jab jaani

Aandhi peechhe jo jal bootha,
prem Hari jan bheena
Kahe Kabir mann bhaya prakaasa,
uday bhaan tam ksheena

~

Na main dharmi na hi adharmi,
na main jati na kaami ho
Na main kehta na main sunta,
na main sevak-swami ho

Na main bandha na main mukta,
na main virat na rangi ho
Na kaahu se nyaara hua,
na kaahu ke sangi ho

Na ham narak lok ko jaate,
na ham swarg sidhaare ho
Sabahi karam hamaaro kiya,
ham karman se nyaare ho

Ya mat ko koi birla boojhe,
so atal ho baitha ho
Mat Kabir kaahu ko thaape,
mat kaahu ko meta ho

~

Santon, sahaj samaadhi bhali
Guru partaap ja din se upji,
surat na ant chali

Aankh na moondun, kaan na roondhun,
kaaya kasht na dhaarun
Khule nain hans hans pehchaanun,
sundar roop nihaarun

Kahun so naam, sunun so sumiran,
khaaun-piyun so pooja
Girah-udyaan eksam dekhun,
bhaav mitaaun dooja

Jahaan jahaan dolun soi parikarma,
jo kuchh karun so seva
Jab soun tab karun dandavat,
poojun aur na deva

Shabad nirantar manva raata,
malin vaasna tyaagi
Uthat-baithat kabahun na chhoote,
aisi taali laagi

Kahe Kabir, sahaj yah rehni
so pargat kar gaai
Sukh-dukh se ek pare param pad,
so pad hai sukhdaai

~

Avadhu, maya taji na jaai
Chhode se vah chhoote naahin,
kotin karai upaai

Girah taj ke bastar baandha,
bastar taj ke pheri
Ladka taj ke chela keenha,
tahun mat maya gheri

Kaam taje tain krodh na jaai,
krodh taje tain lobha
Lobh taje ahankaar na jaai,
maan badhaai shobha

Mann bairaagi maya tyaagi,
shabad mein surat samaai
Kahe Kabir suno bhai saadho,
yah gam birle paai

~

Hansa karo puraatan baat

Kaun des se aaya hansa,
utarna kauno ghaat?
Kahaan hansa bisraam kiya hai,
kahaan lagaaye aas?

Ab hi hansa chet savera,
chalo hamaare saath
Sanshay-shok vahaan nahin vyaapai,
nahin kaal ki traas

Hiyaan madan-ban phool rahe hain,
aave sohan baas
Mann bhaunra jihan urajh rahe hain,
sukh ki na abhilaas

~

Bhakti ka maarag jheena re

Nahin achaah nahin chaahna,
Charnan mein lau leena re

Saadhan keri ras-dhaar mein,
Rahe so nis din bheena re

Raam mein sudh aise base,
Jaise jal mein meena re

Saain sevan mein det sir,
Kuchh bilam na keena re

Kahe Kabir mat bhakti ka,
Pargat kar deena re

≈

Ho santon bhai,
paani mein meen piyaasi
Mohe sun sun aave haansi,
paani mein meen piyaasi

Aatam gyaan bina nar bhatke,
kau Mathura kau Kaasi
Mrig ke naabhi basat kastoori,
ban ban phirat udaasi

Jal bich kamal, kamal bich kaliyaan,
ta par bhanvar nivaasi
So mann vash tirlok bhayo sab,
yati sati sanyaasi

Ja ko dhyaan dhare vidhi harihar,
munijan sahas athaasi
So tere ghat maanhi viraaje,
param purush avinaasi

Hai haajir ko door bataave,
door ki baat niraasi
Kahat Kabira suno bhai saadhu,
guru bina bharam na jaasi

~

Teerath mein sab paani hai,
hove nahin kachhu nahaay dekha

Pratima sakal to jad hai bhai,
bole nahin bolaay dekha

Puraan Qur'an sabai baat hai,
ghat ka parda khol dekha

Anubhav ki baat Kabir kahe,
ye sab hai jhoothi pol dekha

~

Tera mera manva kaise ek hoi re?

Main kehta aankhan ki dekhi,
tu kehta kaagad ki lekhi
Main kehta surjhaavan haari,
tu raakhyo urjhaai re

Main kehta jaagat rahiyo,
tu rehta hai soi re
Main kehta nirmohi rahiyo,
tu jaata hai mohi re

Jugan-jugan samajhaavat haara,
kahi na maanat koi re
Raah bhi andhi chaal bhi andhi,
sab dhan daara khoi re

Satguru dhaara nirmal baahe,
va mein kaaya dhoi re
Kahat Kabir suno bhai saadho,
tab hi vaisa hoi re

≈

Angadhiya deva, kaun kare thaari seva?
Angadhiya deva, koi nahin kare thaari seva

Ghade dev ko sab koi pooje,
nit uth laave seva
Pooran bramha akhandit svaami,
ta ko na jaane bheva

Brahma Vishnu Maheshvar kahiye,
in sir laagi kaai
Inke bharose koi mat rehna,
inhone mukti na paai

Das avataar niranjan kahiye,
so apna nahin hoi
Vo to apni karni bhoge,
karta aur hi koi

Jogi jati tapi sanyaasi,
aap aap mein ladiya
Kahe Kabir suno bhaai saadho,
shabd lakhe so tariya

~

Pandit, baad bade so jhootha
Raam ke kahe jagat gati paave,
to khaand kahe mukh meetha

Paavak kahe paanv jo daahe,
jal kahe trishna bujhaai
Bhojan kahe bhookh jo bhaage,
to duniya tar jaai

Nar ke sang suva Hari bole,
Hari partaap na jaane
Jo kabahu ud jaaye jangal mein,
to Hari surta na aane

Bin dekhe, aras paras bin,
naam liye kya hoi?
Dhan ke kahe dhanik jo hove,
nirdhan rahega na koi

Saachi preet vishay maya se,
Hari bhaktan ko haansi
Kahe Kabir prem nahin upjyo,
baandhe jampur jaasi

~

Saadho, dekho jag bauraana
Saach kaho to maaran dhaave, jhoothe jag patiyaana

Hindu kahat hai Raam hamaara, Musalmaan Rehmaana
Aapas mein dou lade marat hain, maram koi nahin jaana

Bahut mile mohe nemi dharmi, praat karein asnaana
Aatam chhod pashaane pooje, tin ka thotha gyaana

Aasan maar dimbh dhar baithe, mann mein bahut gumaana
Peepar-paathar poojan laage, teerath barat bhulaana

Maala pahire topi pahire, chhap-tilak anumaana
Saakhi sabdai gaavat bhoole, aatam khabar na jaana

Ghar-ghar mantar det phirat hain, mahima ke abhimaana
Guruva sahit shishya sab boode, antakaal pachhtaana

Bahutak dekhe peer auliya, padhein kitaab kuraana
Karein mureed kabar batlaavein, unhun khuda na jaana

Ya vidhi hansat chalat hain hamko, aap kahaavein syaana
Kahe Kabira suno bhai saadho, inmein kaun deewaana?

Na jaane tera saahib kaisa hai

Masjid bheetar mulla pukaare,
kya tera saahib behra hai?
Chyonti ke pag nevar baaje,
so bhi saahib sunta hai

Pandit ho kar aasan maare,
lambi maala japta hai
Antar tere kufar kataari,
yon kya saahib milta hai?

Ooncha neecha mahal banaaya,
gehri neev jamaata hai
Chalne ka mansooba naahin,
rehno ko mann karta hai

Kaudi kaudi maya jodi,
gaadh bhoomi mein dharta hai
Jis lena hai so lai jaaye,
paapi bahi bahi marta hai

Heera paaye parakh nahin jaane,
kaudi parkhan karta hai
Kahe Kabir suno bhai saadho,
Hari jaise ko taisa hai

Sunta nahin dhun ki khabar, anhad ka baaja baajta
Ras mand mandar baajta, baahar sune to kya hua?

Gaanja afeem aur posta bhaang, aur sharaabein peevta
Ek prem ras chaakha nahin, amli hua to kya hua?

Kashi gaya aur Dwarka, teerath sakal bharmat phire
Gaanthi na kholi kapat ki, teerath gaya to kya hua?

Pothi kitaabein vaanchta, auron ko nit samjhaavta
Trikuti mahal khoja nahin, bak bak mara to kya hua?

Kaazi kitaabein kholta, karta naseehat aur ko
Mehram nahin us haal se, kaazi hua to kya hua?

Jogi digambar sevda, kapda range rang laal se
Vaakif nahin us rang se, kapda ranga to kya hua?

Mandir jharokhe raavati gul chaman mein rehte sada
Kehte Kabira hain sahi, har dam mein saahib ram raha

Mann na rangaaye, rangaaye jogi kapda
Mann na phiraaye, phiraaye jogi manka

Aasan maari, jogi, mandir baithaaye
Brahm ne chhaadi poojan laga pathra

Kanva phadaaye, jogi, jata badhaaye
Daadhi rakhaaye ne hoya bakra

Jangal jaaye, jogi, dhuni ramaaye
Raakh lagaaye ne hoya gadhada

Mathva mundaaye, jogi, bhagva rangaaye
Kaam jaraaye ne hoya heejda

Kahe Kabir suno bhai saadho
Jam darvaaje baandhe jaaye pakda

Hamaare Raam Rahim Karim Kesav,
Allah Raam sat soi
Bismil meti Bisambhar ekai,
aur no dooja koi

Inke kaaji mulla peer paigambar,
roja, pachhim nivaaja
Inke poorab disa dev dij pooja,
gyaarasi gang divaaja

Turak maseeti dehure Hindu,
duhutha Raam Khudaai
Jahaan maseeti dehura naahin,
tahaan ka ki thakuraai?

Hindu Turak dou rah tooti,
phooti aru kanraai
Aradh uradh dasahu dis jit tit,
poori rahya Raam raai

Kahai Kabira daas fakira,
apni raah chal bhai
Hindu Turak ka karta ekai,
ta gati lakhi na jaai

～

Loka mati ke bhora re
Jo Kaasi tan tajai Kabir,
to Raamahi kaha nihora re?

Tab ham vaise ab ham aise,
ihai janam ka laaha
Jyon paani paani mil gaihu,
tyon dhuri mile julaaha

Raam bhagti pari ja ko hit chit,
ta ko achraj kaaha
Guru prasaad saadh ki sangat,
jag jeete jaai julaaha

Magahar marai maran nahin paavai,
antai mare Raam lajjaavai
Magahar mare so gadaha hoye
bhal parteet Raam se khoye

Kahai Kabir sunahu re santon,
bhram pare jin koi
Jas Kaasi tas Magahar oosar,
hirdai Raam sat hoi

～

Avadhu, bhajan bhed hai nyaara
Koi jaanega jaananhaara

Kya gaave kya likh batlaave,
kya bharme sansaara?
Kya sandhya tarpan ke keenhe,
jo nahin tatva vichaara?

Moond mundaaye sir jata rakhaaye,
kya tan laaye chhaara?
Kya pooja paahan ki keenhe,
kya phal kiye ahaara?

Bin parichay saahib ho baithe,
vishay ko kare vyavhaara
Gyaan dhyaan ka maram na jaane,
baad kare ahankaara

Agam athaah maha ati gehra,
beej khet nivaara
Maha so dhyaan magan hoi baithe,
kaat karam ki chhaara

Jinke ahaar sada antar mein,
keval tatva vichaara
Kahe Kabir suno ho Gorakh,
taaro sahit parivaara

Gagan ki ot nisaana hai

Dahine soor chandrama baayein
Tin ke beech chhipaana hai

Tan ki kamaan surat ka roda
Shabad baan le taana hai

Maarat baan bheda tan hi tan
Satguru ka parvaana hai

Maaryo baan ghaav nahin tan mein
Jin laaga tin jaana hai

Kahe Kabir suno bhai saadho
Jin jaana tin maana hai

≈

Tu to Raam sumar jag ladne de

Kora kaagaj kaali syaahi,
likhat padhat va ko padhne de

Haathi chalat apni gati mein,
kukkur bhukai to bhukne de

Chandi Bhairav Sitla devi,
dev pujai to pujne de

Kahe Kabir suno bhai saadho,
narak padai va ko padne de

≈

Bhajo re bhaiya
Raam Govind Hari

Jap tap saadhan
kachhu nahin laagat
kharchat nahin gathri

Santat sampat
sukh ke kaaran
ja so bhool padi

Raam naam ko
sumiran kar le
sir pe maut khadi

Kahat Kabira
Raam na ja mukh
ta mukh dhool bhari

≈

Guru se lagan kathin hai bhai
Lagan lage bin kaaj na sarihe,
jeev parlay hoi jaai

Svaati boond liye ratat papihara,
piya piya rat laai
Pyaase praan jaat hain ab hi,
aur neer nahin bhaai

Mirga naad shabad ka bhedi,
shabad sunan ko jaai
Soi shabad suni praan daan de,
tanik na mann mein daraai

Do dal aan jude rann sanmukh,
soora let ladaai
Took took hoi gire dharni pe,
khet chhod nahin jaai

Taji ghar dvaar sati hoi nikli,
satya karan ko jaai
Paavak dekh dare nahin tan ko,
kood pade harshaai

Chhodo apne tan ki aasa,
nirbhay hoi gun gaai
Kahat Kabir aisi lau laave,
sahaj mile guru aai

≈

Avadhu, gagan ghata gehraani

Poorab disa se uthi badariya,
rimjhim barsat paani

Utho gyaani mend sambhaaro,
bahyo jaat yeh paani

Nirat surat ke bail bandhaavo,
jot khet nirbaani
Dubidha doob chhol kar baahar,
bovo naam ki dhaani

Jog jugat se karo rakhvaali,
char na jaave mrig dhaani
Kaatya khet meend ghar laave,
soi kusal kisaani

Paanch sakhi mil kare rasoi,
ek se ek sayaani
Donon thaar baraabar parse,
jeeme muni aur gyaani

Kahe Kabir suno bhai saadho,
yeh pad hai nirbaani
Jo ya pad ko parichay paave,
ta ko naam vigyaani

~

Raam ras meetho ghano re, jogiya ji
Piye amar hoi jaaye

Main mera ghar jaadiya re, jogiya ji
liyo paleeta haath
Koi agar jaado ghar aapro re, jogiya ji
chalo hamaare saath

Ghar jaadyo ghar ubhre re, jogiya ji
ghar raakhyo ghar jaaye
Ek achambho main dekhiyo re, jogiya ji
mado kaal ne khaaye

Aage re aage dav jade re, jogiya ji
peechhe hariya hoye
Balihaari un roonkhdi re, jogiya ji
jad kaatyo phal hoye

Dhruv piyo, Prahlad piyo re, jogiya ji
piyo Peepe Ravidas
Bhagat Kabira ras pi rahyo re, jogiya ji
phir peevan ri aas

≈

Thaaro Raam hirday mein,
baahar kyon bhatke?

Aisa aisa heerla ghat mein kahiye
Jauhari bina heera kaun parkhe?

Aisa aisa ghrit doodh mein kahiye
Mathiye bina maakhan kaise nikle?

Aisa madhur ras ookh mein bhariya
Piliye bina ras kaise nikle?

Aisi aisi aag lakdi mein kahiye
Ghasiye bina aag kaise nikle?

Aisa aisa kivaad hivde pe jadiya
Gura bina taala kaun khole?

Kahat Kabir suno bhai saadho
Raam na mile thaane bin atke

~

Ber chalya mera bhai,
magan hoi, ber chalya mera bhai
Raam naam ro gelo pakdo,
chhodo ni moorkhaai

Pehle to guruji ham janmya,
peechhe bada bhai
Dhoom dhaam se pita janmya,
sabse peechhe maai

Pehle to guruji doodh jamaayo,
peechhe gaay no doi
Bachhda un re rame pet mein,
ghrit bechva gayi

Keedi chaali saasre,
nau mann surmo saath
Haathi un re haath mein,
oont lapetya jaai

Eenda hata bolta,
bachiya bolya naai

Kahat Kabir sun bhai saadho,
moorakh samjhe naai

∽

Avadhu, kudrat ki gat nyaari
Rank nivaaj karai vah raaja,
bhoopati karai bhikhaari

Ye te lavangahi phal nahin laagai,
chandan phool na phoolai
Machh shikaari ramai jangal mein,
sinh samudrahi jhoolai

Reda rookh bhaya malayaagir,
chahun dis phooti baasa
Teen lok bramhaand khand mein,
dekhai andh tamaasa

Pangul meru sumer unlanghai,
tribhuvan mukta dolai
Goonga gyaan-vigyaan prakaasai,
anhad baani bolai

Baandhi akaas pataal pathaave,
ses sarag par raajai
Kahai Kabir Raam hain raaja,
jo kuchh karein so chhaajai

∽

Avadhu, aisa gyaan vichaar
Bhere chadhe so adhadhar doobe,
niradhaar bhaye paar

Aughat chale so nagri pahunche,
baat chale te loote
Ek jevari sab laptaane,
ke baandhe ke chhoote

Mandir pesi chahun disi bheege,
baahar rahe to sookha
Sari maare to sada sukhaare,
an-maare se dookha

Bin nainan ke sab jag dekhe,
lochan rehte andha
Kahe Kabir kuchh samajh padi hai,
ye jag dekha dhandha

Ek achambha dekha re bhai,
thaada sinh charaave gaai

Pehle poot peechhe bhayi maai,
chela ke guru laage paai

Jal ki machhli taruvar byaai,
pakdi bilaai murgai khaai

Bailahi daar goni ghar aai,
kutta ku le gayi bilaai

Tali kar shaakha upar kari mool,
bahut bhaanti jad laage phool

Kahe Kabir ya pad ko boojhe,
ta ko teenyo tribhuvan soojhe

～

Dariyaav ka lahar dariyaav hai ji
Dariya aur lahar mein bhinn koyam?

Uthe to neer hai, baithe to neer hai
Kaho ji doosra kis tarah hoyam?

Usi ke naam ko pher ke lahar dhara
Lahar ke kahe kya neer khoyam?

Jagat hi ke pher sab, jagat parabramha mein
Gyaan kar dekh Kabir goyam

～

Inka bhed bata mere avadhu,
achhi karni kar le tu
Daali phool jagat ke maanhi,
jahaan dekhun vahaan tu ka tu

Haathi mein haathi ban baitho,
keedi mein hai chhoto tu

Hoye mahaavat upar baithe,
haankan vaala tu ka tu

Choron ke sang chori karta,
badmaashon mein bhedo tu,
Chori karke tu bhag jaave,
pakadne vaala tu ka tu

Daata ke sang daata ban jaaye,
bhikhaari mein bhedo tu
Mangto hokar maangan laage,
dene vaala tu ka tu

Nar naari mein ek viraaje,
do duniya mein deese kyon?
Baalak hokar rovan laage,
raakhan vaala tu ka tu

Jal thal jeev mein tu hi viraaje,
jahaan dekhun vahaan tu ka tu
Kahe Kabir suno bhai saadhu,
guru mila hai jyon ka tyon

~

Ghat ghat mein panchhi bolta

Aap hi dandi aap taraaju,
aap hi baitha tolta

Aap hi maali aap bagicha,
aap hi kaliyaan todta

Sab mein sab ban aap biraaje,
jad chetan mein dolta

Kahat Kabira suno bhai saadho,
mann ki kundi kholta

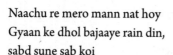

Naachu re mero mann nat hoy
Gyaan ke dhol bajaaye rain din,
sabd sune sab koi

Raahu Ketu navgrah naache
Jampur anand hoy
Giri samundar dharti naache
Lok naache hans-roi

Chhaapa tilak lagaaye baans chadhi
Hoi rahu jag se nyaara
Sahas kala kar mann mero naache
Reejhe sirjanhaara

Jo tum kood jaao bhavsaagar
Kala badaiya mein tero
Kahe Kabir, suno bhai saadho
Ho rahu satguru chero

Mann laago mero yaar fakiri mein
Mann laago mero yaar gareebi mein

Jo sukh paaya Raam bhajan mein
Vo sukh naahin ameeri mein

Haath mein tumbi bagal mein sota
Chaaron disha jaageeri mein

Bhala bura sab ka sun leejiye
Kar guzraan gareebi mein

Prem nagar mein rahani hamaari
Bhali ban aayi saboori mein

Aakhir yeh tan khaak milega
Kaahe phirat magroori mein?

Kahe Kabir suno bhai saadho
Saahib mile hain saboori mein

~

Mann mast hua phir kya bole?

Heera paaya baandh gathadiya
Baar baar va ko kyon khole?

Halki thi jab chadhi taraazu
Poori bhayi phir kyon tole?

Surat kalaalan bhayi matwaali
Madva pi gayi antole

Hansa nhaave maansarovar
Taal talaiya mein kyon dole?

Tera saahib hai tujh maanhi
Baahar naina kyon khole?

Kahe Kabir, suno bhai saadho
Saahib mil gaya til ole

≈

Dhun sun ke manva magan hua ji

Laagi samaadhi guru charana ji
Ant sakha dukh door hua ji

Saar shabad ek dori laagi
Te chadh hansa paar hua ji

Shoonya shikhar par jhaalar jhalke
Barsat amiras prem chuva ji

Kahe Kabira suno bhai saadho
Chaakh chaakh al-mast hua ji

≈

Naiharva hamka na bhaavai

Saain ki nagari param ati sundar,
jahaan koi jaay na aavai
Chaand sooraj jahaan pavan na paani,
ko sandes pahunchaavai
Darad yah saain ko sunaavai?

Aage chalo panth nahin soojhe,
peechhe dosh lagaavai
Kehi vidhi sasure jaaun mori sajni,
viraha jor jaraavai
Vishay ras naach nachaavai

Bin satguru apno nahin koi
jo yah raah bataavai
Kahat Kabira suno bhai saadho,
sapne na peetam aavai
Tapan yah jiya ki bujhaavai

∽

Tadpe bin baalam mora jiya

Din naahin chain, rain naahin nindiya
Tadap tadap ke bhor kiya

Tan mann more rahat as dole
Sooni sej par janam chhiya

Nain thakit rahe panth na soojhe
Saain bedardi sudh na liya

Kahat Kabir suno bhai saadho
Haro peer dukh jor jiya

~

Rehna nahin des veeraana hai
Yahaan rehna nahin des begaana hai

Yeh sansaar kaagad ki pudiya
Boond pade ghul jaana hai

Yeh sansaar kaanton ki baadi
Yahaan ulajh-pulajh mar jaana hai

Yeh sansaar jhaad aur jhaakad
Aag lage jal jaana hai

Kahat Kabir suno bhai saadho
Satguru gyaan thikaana hai

~

Koi nahin apna,
samajh mana

Dhan daulat tera maal khajeena,
do din ka sapna

Nanga aana, nanga jaana,
nahin kapda rakhna

Trikuti mein se jaan nikal gayi,
munh per daalo dhakna

Chaar jan mil ke khatiya uthaana,
jangal beech rakhna

Jangal mein laayi lakad ki mauli,
koi un se phoonkna

Kahat Kabira suno bhai saadho,
vo hi hai ghar apna

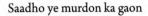

Saadho ye murdon ka gaon

Peer mare, paigambar mari hain,
mari hain zinda jogi
Raaja mari hain, parja mari hain,
mari hain baid aur rogi

Chanda mari hai, sooraj mari hai,
mari hain dharni aakaasa
Chaudah bhuvan ke chaudhari mari hain
inhun ki ka aasa?

Nauhu mari hain, dasahu mari hain,
mari hain sahas atthaasi
Taintees koti devta mari hain,
padi kaal ki phaansi

Naam anaam anant rahat hai,
dooja tatva na hoi
Kahe Kabir suno bhai saadho
bhatak maro mat koi

≈

Ud jaayega hans akela,
jag darshan ka mela

Jaise paat gire taruvar ke,
milna bahut duhela
Na jaanun kidhar girega,
lagya pavan ka rela

Jab hove umar poori,
jab chhootega hukum hujoori
Jam ke doot bade majboot,
jam se pada jhamela

Das Kabir har ke gun gaave,
va har ko paar na paave
Guru ki karni guru jaayega,
chele ki karni chela

≈

Mann phoola phoola phire,
jagat mein kaisa naata re?

Maata kahe yeh putra hamaara, bahin kahe bir mera
Bhai kahe yeh bhuja hamaari, naari kahe nar mera

Pet pakari ke maata rove, baanh pakari ke bhai
Lapat jhapat ke tiriya rove, hans akela jaai

Jab lag jeeve maata rove, bahin rove das maasa
Terah din tak tiriya rove, phir khoje ghar baasa

Chaargaji chargaji mangaayi, chadha kaath ki ghodi
Chaaron kone aag lagaayi, phoonk diyo jas hori

Haad jare jas ban ki lakadiya, kes jare jas ghaasa
Sona jaisi kaaya jar gayi, koi na aayo paasa

Ghar ki tiriya dekhan laagi, phiri chahun deesa
Kahe Kabir suno bhai saadho, chhaado jag ki aasa

Zara halke gaadi haanko,
mere Raam gaadi vaale
Zara dheere dheere gaadi haanko,
mere Raam gaadi vaale

Gaadi meri rang rangeeli,
paiya hai laal gulaal
Haankan vaali chhail-chhabeeli,
baithan vaala Raam

Gaadi atki ret mein,
aur majal padi hai door
Dharmi dharmi paar utar gaya,
paapi chaknachoor

Des des ka vaid bulaaya,
laaya jadi aur booti
Va jadi booti tere kaam na aayi
jad Raam ke ghar se chhooti

Chaar jana mil mato uthaayo,
baandhi kaath ki ghodi
Le ja ke marghat pe rakhiya,
phoonk deeni jaise Holi

Bilakh bilakh kar tiriya rove,
bichhad gayi meri jodi
Kahe Kabir suno bhai saadho,
jin jodi tin todi

~

Saadho yeh tan thaat tambure ka

Ainchat taar marodat khoonti
Niksat raag hajoore ka

Toota taar bikhar gayi khoonti
Ho gaya dhooram-dhoore ka

Ya dehi ka garab na keejai
Ud gaya hans tambure ka

Kahe Kabir suno bhai saadho
Agam panth koi soore ka

～

Guruji ne diyo amar naam,
guru sareekha koi nahin
Alakh bharya hai bhandaar,
kami ja mein hai nahin

Naam sareekho yo daan,
mati do ajaan ne
Ghughu dekhe taara handi jyot,
vo kai jaane bhaan ne

Kharche se khootya nahin,
jalaaya se na jale
Aisa vaancho ved puraan,
naam guru bina na mile

Ugya jal thal bhaan,
chaand taara chhipi gaya
Aisa jap tap yog anek,
naam tale dabi gaya

Chitvan chit achet,
rato nij naam ne

Ghat bheetar saahib, Kabir
chalo nij dhaam ne

~

Ham pardesi panchhi baba,
ani des ra naai
Ani des ra log acheta,
pal pal par pachhtaai

Mukh bin bolna pag bin chalna,
bina pankh ud jaai
Bina moh ki surat hamaari,
anhad mein ram jaai

Chhaaya baithun to agni vyaapai,
dhoop adhik sitlaai
Chhaaya dhoop se satguru nyaara,
ham satguru ke maai

Aathon pahar adag rahe aasan,
kade na utre saai
Mann pavan donon nahin pahunche,
uni des ke maai

Nirgun roop hai mere daata,
sirgun naam dharaai
Kahe Kabir milo nirgun se,
ajar amar ho jaai

~

Avadhoota, yugan yugan ham yogi
Aavai na jaay mitai na kabahun,
sabad anaahat bhogi

Sabhi thaur jamaat hamari,
sab hi thaur par mela
Ham sab maay sab ham maay,
ham hai bahuri akela

Ham hi siddh samaadhi ham hi,
ham mauni ham bole
Roop saroop aroop dikha ke,
ham hi mein ham to khele

Kahe Kabira jo suno bhai saadho,
naahin na koi ichchha
Apni madhi mein aap main dolun,
khelun sahaj sva-ichchha

Sakhi va ghar sabse nyaara,
jahaan pooran purush hamaara

Jahaan na sukh dukh, saach jhooth nahin,
paap na punya pasaara
Nahin din rain, chaand nahin sooraj,
bin jyoti ujiyaara

Na tahaan gyaan dhyaan, na jap tap,
ved kiteb na baani

Karni dharni rehni gehni,
ye sab vahaan hiraani

Dhar nahin adhar, na baahar bheetar,
pind bramhaand kachhu naahin
Paanch tatva gun teen nahin tahaan,
saakhi shabd na taahin

Mool na phool, beli nahin beeja,
bina brikchh phal sohe
Oham soham ardh urdh nahin,
svaasa lekhan kohe

Nahin nirgun na sirgun bhai,
na sooksham asthoola
Nahin akshar nahin avigat hoi,
ye sab bhram ke moola

Jahaan purush tahvaan kachhu naahin,
kahe Kabir ham jaana
Hamri sain lakhe jo koi,
paave pad nirvaana

～

Maya maha thagani ham jaani
Tirgun phaans liye kar dole,
bole madhuri baani

Kesav ke Kamla hoy baithi,
Shiv ke bhavan Bhavaani

Panda ke moorat hoy baithi,
teerath mein bhayi paani

Yogi ke yogin hoy baithi,
raaja ke ghar raani
Kaahu ke heera hoy baithi,
kaahu ke kaudi kaani

Bhaktan ke bhaktin hoy baithi,
Bramha ke bramhaani
Kahe Kabir suno bhaai saadho,
ye sab akath kahaani

～

Nirbhay nirgun gun re gaaunga

Mool kamal dridh aasan baandhun ji
Ulti pavan chadhaaunga

Mann mamta ko thir kar laaun ji
Paanchon tatva milaaunga

Ingla pingla sukhman naadi ji
Tirveni pe nhaaunga

Paanch pancheeso pakad mangaaun ji
Ek hi dor lagaaunga

Shoonya shikhar par anhad baaje ji
Raag chhatees sunaaunga

Kahat Kabira suno bhai saadho ji
Jeet nishaan ghuraaunga

Koi sunta hai guru gyaani,
gagan mein aavaaj hove jheeni

Pehle aaya naad bind se,
peechhe jamaaya paani
Sab ghat pooran poor rahya hai,
alakh purush nirbaani

Vahaan se aaya patta likhaaya,
trishna to un ne bujhaani
Amrit chhod vishay ras peeve,
ulti phaans phansaani

Bin dharti ek mandal deese,
bin sarovar jyon paani
Gagan mandal mein hoye ujiyaala,
bole gurumukh baani

Gagan mandal mein gau biyaani,
dharni pe doodh jamaaya
Maakhan maakhan santon ne khaaya,
chhaachh jagat bapraani

Oham soham baaja baaje,
trikuti dhaam suhaani

Ingla pingla sukhman joya,
sunn mein dhwaja phehraani

Din bhar jo najar bhar dekhe,
ajar amar nishaani
Kahe Kabir suno bhaai saadho,
gaai agam ki baani

~

Jhagda ek navero Raam,
je tum apne jan su kaam

Bramha bada ki jahaan se aaya,
bed bada ki jin upjaaya?

Mann bada ki jehi mann maane,
Raam bada ki Raamahi jaane?

Kahe Kabir hun khada udaas,
teerath bade ki Hari ke daas?

Dohas

Kabira khada bazaar mein, liye lukaathi haath
Jo ghar jaare aapna, chalo hamaare saath.

Kabir khada baazaar mein, sab ki maange khair
Na kaahu se dosti, na kaahu se bair.

Kabira jab ham paida hue, to jag hanse ham roye
Aisi karni kar chalo, ham hanse jag roye.

Kaal kare so aaj kar, aaj kare so ab
Pal mein parlay hoigi, bahuri karega kab?

Chalti chaaki dekh kar, diya Kabira roye
In do paatan ke beech mein, saabut bacha na koi.

Maati kahe kumhaar se, tu kya roondat mohe?
Ik din aisa aayega, main roondungi tohe.

Maala kahe hai kaath ki, tu kya pherat mohe?
Mann ka manka pher de, turat mila dun tohe.

Aisi vaani boliye, mann ka aapa khoye
Auran ko sheetal kare, aapahu sheetal hoye.

Masi kaagad chhuo nahin, kalam gahyo nahin haath
Chaar jugaan ra mahaatm, Kabir mukh se janaai baat.

Pothi padh padh jag muaan, pandit bhaya na koi
Dhai aakhar prem ka, padhe so pandit hoye.

Padhi padhi ke patthar bhayo, likhi likhi bhayo hai eent
Kahe Kabir tohe prem ki, laagi na ekai chheent.

Likha likhi ki hai nahin, dekha dekhi baat
Dulha dulhan mil gaye, to pheeki padi baaraat.

Jaat na poochho saadhu ki, poochh leejiye gyaan
Mol karo talwaar ka, padi rehne do myaan.

Guru Govind donon khade, ka ke laagun paaye?
Balihaari Gurudev ki, jine Govind diyo bataaye.

Jab main tha tab Hari nahin, ab Hari hai main naahin
Prem gali ati saankri, ya mein dou samaaye naahin.

Bura jo dekhan main gaya, bura na milya koi
Jo tan khoja aapna, to mujhse bura na koi.

Kabir teri jhonpdi, gal katan ke paas
Karanta so bharanta, tu kyun phire udaas?

Karni kare to kyun dare, kar hi kyun pachhtaaye?
Tu ne boya ped babool ka, phir aam kahaan se khaaye?

Kabir aap thagaaiye, aur na thagve koi
Aap thage sukh oopje, aur thage dukh hoi.

Chaah gayi chinta miti, manva beparvaah
Jisko kachhu nahin chaahiye, so hi shehenshah.

Dheere dheere re mana, dheere sab kuchh hoye
Maali seenche sau ghada, ritu aaye phal hoye.

Ek saadhe sab sadhe, sab saadhe ek jaaye
Maali seenche mool ko, to phoole phale aghaaye.

Saain itna deejiye, ja mein kutumb samaaye
Main bhi bhookha na rahun, saadhu na bhookha jaaye.

Kabir kahe Kamaal se, do baatein seekh le
Kar saahib ki bandagi, bhookhe ko ann de.

Kabir Kabir kya karo, socho aap shareer
Jo tan khoja aapna, to aapahu daas Kabir.

Kabir mann nirmal bhaya, jaise Ganga neer
Peechhe peechhe Hari phire, kahat Kabir Kabir.

Jyon tilli mein tel hai, jyon chakmak mein aag
Tera saain tujh mein hai, tu jaag sake to jaag.

Kabir kuaan ek hai, panihaari anek
Bartan sabke nyaare hain, par paani sab mein ek.

Boond padi samoond mein, jaane hai sab koi
Samoond samaana boond mein, jaane birla koi.

Saahib tamaari saahibi, sab ghat rahi samaaye
Jyon mehendi ke paat mein, laali lakhi nahin jaaye.

Laali mere laal ki, jit dekhun tit laal
Laali dekhan main gayi, to main bhi ho gayi laal.

Laal laal sab koi kahe, aur sabke palle laal
Gaanth khol dekha nahin, ya se bhaya kangaal.

Tan matki mann jherna, surat bilovanhaar
Maakhan Kabira kha gaya, chhaachh piyo sansaar.

Bada hua to kya hua, jaise ped khajoor
Panthi ko chhaaya nahin, phal laage ati door.

Bada badaai na kare, bada na bole bol
Heera mukh se na kahe, ki laakh hamaara mol.

Oonche paani na tike, vo to neeche hi thehraaye
Jo nar ooncha ho raha, so pyaasa hi mar jaaye.

Jaati julaaha kya kare, hirday base Gopal
Kabir Raamaiya kanth milu, chookahi sab janjaal.

Jaati ke abhimaan mein bhool raha sansaar
Bin parichay sadguru ke, chaaron varan chamaar.

Raam bhajan bhajyo nahin, nahin kiyo Hari su het
Ab pachhtaaya kya phire, jab chidiya chug gayi khet?

Hindu mue hain Raam kahi, Musalmaan Khudaai
Kahe Kabir so jeevta, dui mein kadai na jaai.

Paahan pooje Hari mile, toh main poojun pahaad
Ta se toh chakki bhali, pees khaaye sansaar.

Kankar patthar jod ke masjid liyo chunaaye
Ta chadh Mullah baang de, kya behra hua Khudaai?

Kesa kya bigaadiya, jo moonde sau baar
Mann ko kaahe na moondiye, ja mein vishay vikaar?

Jogi jugat jaane nahin, kapda ranga to kya hua?
Mann ka kufar toota nahin, qalma padha to kya hua?

Kabir ya sansaar ko, samjhaaya sau baar
Poonchh pakde bhed ki, utarna chaahe paar.

Kabir ka ghar shikhar pe, silhali se gel
Paanv na tike papeel ka, kyon pandit laade bail?

Vakta gyaani jagat mein, pandit kavi anant
Satya padaarath paarkhi, birla koi sant.

Pindat boro patra, qaazi chhod Quran
Vo taareeq bataai de, jab the na zameen aasmaan.

Pindat aur masaalchi, donon soojhe naahin
Auron ko kare chaandni, aap andhere maanhi.

Kabir pustak padh padh ke, ast pada sansaar
Peed na upji preet ki, to kyon kar kare pukaar?

Laagi laagi sab kahein, laagi buri bala
Laagi to tab jaaniyo, jab aar paar hui jaaye.

Aaye ek hi des se, ne utre ek hi ghaat
Beech mein taati bharam ki, to ho gaye baarah baat.

Kabir gudadi beekhari, sauda gaya bikaaye
Khota baandha gaanthadi, khara liya nahin jaaye.

Kabir kaljug aaviyo, sant nahin maane koi
Kooda kapti laalchi, un ri pooja hoye.

Kabira tu haara bhala, jeetan de sansaar
Jeete ko jam le jaayega, haara Hari ke dwaar.

Fikr sab ko kha gayi, fikr sab ka peer
Fikr ki jo phaanki kare, va ko naam fakir.

Nindak niyare raakhiye, aangan kuti chhavaaye
Bin saabun paani bina, nirmal kare subhaaye.

Hirday maanhi aarsi, aur mukh dekha nahin jaaye
Mukh to tab hi dekhiye, jab dil ki duvidha jaaye.

Mann ke mate mat chaaliye, mann jiyaan tiyaan lai jaaye
Mann ko aisa maariye, mann tukda tukda hui jaaye.

Mann lobhi, mann laalchi, mann chanchal mann chor
Mann ke mate mat chaaliye, mann palak palak mein aur.

Mann ke mate mat chaaliye, mann ke mate anek
Jo mann par asvaar rahe, so saadhu koi ek.

Mann ke haare haar hai, mann ke jeete jeet
Mann milaave Raam se, mann hi kare hai fajeet.

Mann mari mamta mari, mar mar gaye shareer
Aasha trishna na mari, keh gaye daas Kabir.

Daudat daudat daudiya, jahaan lag mann ki daud
Daud thake mann thir bhaya, to vastu thor ki thor.

Jitni leher samoond mein, utni mann ki daud
Sahaje moti neepje, jab mann aave hai thor.

Surta phansi sansaar mein, yahaan se pad gaya door
Surat baandh kar sthir karo, to aathon peher hazoor.

Shabad bina surti aandhri, kaho kahaan ko jaaye?
Dwaar na paave shabd ka, phir phir bhatki khaaye.

Moti maya sab taje, jheeni taje na koi
Peer paigambar auliya, jheeni sab ko khaaye.

Jheeni maya jin taje, moti gayi bilaaye
Kahe Kabir ta daas ke, sab dukh gaye hiraaye.

Jaagan hi mein sovna, sovan hi mein raag
Ek to ban mein ghar kare, doojo ghar mein rahe beraag.

Svaans svaans mein naam le, virtha svaans mat khoye
Na jaane is svaans ka phir aavan hoye na hoye.

Svaansa ki kar sumirani, kar ajapa ko jaap
Param tatva ko dhyaan dharo, to sohang aapo aap.

Sohang poya pavan mein, baandho surat sumer
Brahm gaanth hirday dharo, is vidh maala pher.

Maala hai nij svaans ki, pherega koi daas
Chauraasi bharme nahin, kate kaal ki phaans.

Saadhu aisa chaahiye, dukhe dukhaave naahin
Paan phool chhede nahin, par rahe baag ke maanhi.

Kabir bahut bhatkiya, mann le vishay viraam
Chaalat chaalat jug bhaya, aur til ke ote Raam.

Kabir padhna door kar, pustak dei bahaaye
Baavan aakhar chhod kar, rarai mamai chit laaye.

Raag Raam ko roop hai, aur Raam raag ke maanhi
Sambhaar ke suna karo, aur dikhne mein kachhu naahin.

Sab van to tulsi bhaye aur parvat Shaligram
Sab nadiyaan Ganga bhayin, jab jaana aatam Raam.

Rag rag mein bole Raam ji, aur rom rom rarankaar
Sahaje hi dhun upje, so hi sumiran saar.

Maala japun na kar japun, aur mukh se kahun na Raam
Raam hamaara hamein jape, ham paayo bisraam.

Raam naam ki loot hai, loot sake to loot
Ant kaal pachhtaayega, jab praan jaayega chhoot.

Raam naam ki khoonti gaadhi, sooraj taana tanta
Chadhte utarte dam ki khabar le, phir nahin aana banta.

Heera pada baazaar mein, khalak ulaanghya jaaye
Jab aavega paarkhi, sahaje lega uthaaye.

Kabir kamaai aapni, kabahun na nishfal jaaye
Saat samudra aada phire, par mile agaadi aaye.

Kabir naav jarjari, aur koode khevanhaar
Halke halke tiri gaye, boode jin sar bhaar.

Main meri jab jaayegi, tab aavegi aur
Jab mann nishchal bhaya, tab paavega thor.

Jab lag meri, meri kare, tab lag kaaj ekai na sare
Jab meri, meri mati jaaye, tab Hari kaaj savaare aaye.

Mera mujh mein kuchh nahin, jo kuchh hai so tera
Tera tujh ko saunp dun, kya laagat hai mera?

Jo kuchh kiya so tum kiya, bande se kachhu naahin
Kahun jo ki main kiya, to tum hi the mujh maanhi.

Kathni meethi khaand si, karni vish ki loi
Kathni se karni mile, to vish se amrit hoi.

Sahaj sahaj sab koi kahe, sahaj na cheenhe koi
Jin sahaje Hari mile, sahaj kaheeje soi.

Hai kou sant sahaj sukh upje, jaako jap-tap deun dalaali
Ek boond bhari Raam ras, jyon bhari deyi kalaali.

Kasturi kundal base, mrig dhoondhe ban maanhi
Aise ghat ghat mein Raam hai, moorakh samjhe naahin.

Laalan ki nahin boriyaan, hansan ke nahin paat
Singhan ke nahin lehere, aur sadhu na chale jamaat.

Ochhi talaai bug ghano, avsar aayo hans
Mat kar talaai gaarbo, tu samdarvaasi hans.

Jin khoja tin paaiya, gehre paani peth
Hun baura dooban daryo, to raha kinaare baith.

Gagan mandal ke beech mein, jahaan jhalke hai noor
Nugura mahal na paaviya, pahunchega koi soor.

Vastu kahaan dhoondhe kahaan, aur kai vidhi aave haath?
Vastu thikaane paaiye, jad bhedi leenha saath.

Dharni to kaagaz karun, lekhan karun ban raaye
Saat samandar masi karun, guru gun likha na jaaye.

Yeh tan vish ki beladi, guru amrit ki khaan
Sheesh diye aur guru mile, to bhi sasta jaan.

Haan kahun to hai nahin, na bhi kahyo nahin jaaye
Haan aur na ke beech mein, mera satguru raha samaaye.

Guru hamaara gagan mein, chela hai chit maanhi
Surat shabad mela bhaya, kabahu bichhadat naahin.

Guru kumhaar shishya kumbh hai, gadh gadh kaadhe khot
Antar haath sahaar de, aur baahar maare chot.

Satguru chadhe shikaar pe, haath mein laal kabaan
Moorakh moorakh bach gaye, koi maara sant sujaan.

Koi maare top teer se, aave dwaadas ghaav
Mere satguru maare shabad se, tal mundi ne upar paanv.

Satguru mera baaniya, kar raha banaj bepaar
Bin takdi bin paalne, tol raha sansaar.

Ek daal do panchhi baitha, ek guru ek chela
Chela vo jo phal-phool khaave, guru nirantar khela.

Ye sab guru hain had ke, behad ke guru naahin
Behad aapo upje, anubhav ke ghar maanhi.

Kanphoonka guru had ka, behad ka guru aur
Jab behad ka guru mile, tab lage thikaana thor.

Kabir soi peer hai, jo jaane par peed
Jo par peed na jaanta, so kaafir be-peer.

Kabir ki baani atpati, jhatpat lakhi na jaaye
Jo jhatpat se lakhi le, va ki khatpat hi mati jaaye.

Dharti to roti bhayi, aur kaaga liye jaaye
Koi poochho apne guru se, vo kahaan baith kar khaaye.

Jab lag sinh rahe ban maanhi, tab lag ye ban phoole naahin
Ulta siyaal sinh ko khaai, tab ye phoole sab banraai.

Hindu kaho to hoon nahin, Musalmaan bhi naahin
Gaibi donon deen mein, khelun donon maanhi.

Raam Rahima ek hai, mat samjho koi do
Andar taati bharam ki, ja se soojhe do.

Raam Rahima ek hai, aur Kaaba Kashi ek
Maida ek pakvaan bahu, baith Kabira dekh.

Kaaba phir Kashi bhaya, aur Raam hi bhaya Rahim
Mot choon maida bhaya, aur baith Kabira jeem.

Ek Raam Dashrath ka beta, dooja ghat ghat mein baitha
Teeje Raam ka sakal pasaara, chautha sabhi se nyaara.

Tu tu karta tujh gaya, mujh mein rahi na hun
Vaara pheri bali gayi, jit dekhun tit tu.

Sab ghat mora saaiyaan, sooni sej na koi
Balihaari una ghat ki, vo ja ghat parghat hoye.

Ye to ghar hai prem ka, khaala ka ghar naahin
Sheesh kaat bhoun dhare, tab baithe ghar maanhi.

Prem piyaala so piye, jo sheesh dakshina de
Lobhi sheesh na de sake, vo naam prem ka le.

Chaakho chaahe prem ras, raakho chaahe maan
Do khadag aur ek myaan, dekha suna nahin kaan.

Prem prem sab koi kahe, prem na cheenhe koi
Aghat prem pinjar base, prem kahaave soi.

Ja ghat prem na sanchare, va ghat jaan smashaan
Jaise khaal lohaar ki, jo svaans let bin praan.

Prem na baadi upje, prem na haat bikaaye
Bina prem ka maanava, bandhiya jampur jaaye.

Ghaayal ki gati aur hai, auran ki gati aur
Jab prem baan hirday laga, tab raha thikaane thor.

Prem chhipaaya na chhipe, ja ghat pargat hoye
Agar mukh se bole nahin, to nain det hain roye.

Jal mein base kumudini, aur chanda base aakaash
Jo ja ke hirday base, vo va hi ke paas.

Preetam ke pattiyaan likhun, jo vo base vides
Tan mein mann mein nainan mein, ta ko kaun sandes?

Nainon antar aav tu, naina jhanp tohe lun
Na main dekhun aur ko, na tohe dekhan dun.

Nainon ki kar kothri, putli sej bichhaaye
Palkon ki chik daar ke, piya liya rijhaaye.

Akhiyan prem basaiya, jin jaane dukhdaai
Naam snehi kaarane, ro ro rain bitaai.

Nainan to jhari laaiya, rahat bahe nis baas
Papeeha jyon piyu piyu kare, piya milan ki aas.

Kaaga sab tan khaaiyo, chun chun khaaiyo maas
Ye do naina mat khaaiyo, mohe piya milan ki aas.

Saajan aaya main sunya, kaisi jugat karaan?
Thaal bharaana motiye, us par nain dharaan.

Saajan phool gulaab ro, to main phoolaan ri baas
Saajan mhaaro kaaljo, to main saajan ro saans.

Saajan saajan main karaan, aur saajan jeev jadi
Choodala maanhi maandna, to nirkhaan ghadi ghadi.

Saajan ham tum ek hain, bas kahan sunan ko do
Mann ko mann se toliye, to do mann kabhi na ho.

Akath kahaani prem ki, kachhu kahi nahin jaai
Goonge keri sarkara, baithe muskaai.

Yeh tan kaacha kumbh hai, liye phire the saath
Thapka laaga phooti gaya, kachhu nahin aaya haath.

Phoolya phaalya kya phire, kya batlaavat ang?
Ik din fanaa ho jaayega, jaise keet patang.

Kabir gaafil kyon phire, aur kyon sove ghanghor
Tere sirhaane jam khada, jyon andhiyaare chor.

Aaya hai sab jaayega, raaja rank fakeer
Koi singhaasan chadhi chale, koi bandhe zanjeer.

Jo uge so aathme, phoole so kumlaaye
Jo choone so dhahi pade, janme so mari jaaye.

Jo marne se jag dare, so mere mann anand
Kabahu marihun, kabahu paaihun, pooran paramanand.

Marta marta jag muaan, mar bhi na jaane koi
Aisi marni mar chalo, phir na marna hoi.

Kabir bhaati kalaal ki, bahutak baithe aaye
Sir saunpe soi piye, nahin to piya na jaaye.

Ooncha taruvar gagan phal, aur birla panchhi khaaye
Va ko to vo hi bhake, jo jeete ji mar jaaye.

Main marjeeva samudra ka, dubki maari ek
Mutthi laaya gyaan ki, ta mein vastu anek.

Shabd kahaan se uthta, kaho kahaan ko jaaye?
Haath paanv va ke nahin, phir kaise pakda jaaye?

Naabhi-kamal se uthta, shoonya mein jaaye samaaye
Haath paanv va ke nahin, vo surat se pakda jaaye.

Tan thir mann thir vachan thir, surat nirat thir hoye
Kahe Kabir va pal ko, kalp na paave koi.

Naam ratat mann sthir bhaya, gyaan kathat bhaya leen
Surat shabad ekai bhaya, jal hi ho gayi meen.

Paani se bhi paatla, dhuen se bhi jheen
Pavan se utaavla, dost Kabira keenh.

Bin paavan ka panth hai, bin basti ka des
Bina pind ka purush hai, kahe Kabir sandes.

Jahaan na cheenti chadh sake, raai na thehraai
Mann pavana ki gam nahin, tahaan Kabir lau laai.

Ghaate paani sab bhare, aughat bhare na koi
Aughat ghaat Kabir ka, bhare so nirmal hoye.

Jaat hamaari aatma, praan hamaara naam
Alakh hamaara isht hai, aur gagan hamaara gaam.

Baagon na ja re, teri kaaya mein gulzaar
Asht kamal pe baith ke, tu dekhe roop apaar.

Avval Allah noor upaaya, kudrat ke sab bande
Ek noor se jag upaajya, ko bhale ko mande?

Main laga us ek se, ek bhaya sab maanhi
Sab mera main saban ka, tahaan doosra naahin.

Sab par teri saahibi, tujh par saahib naahin
Niraakaar nirbhay tu hi, aur sakal bhar maanhi.

Had mein baitha kathat hai, behad ki gam naahin
Behad ki gam hoyegi, tab kuchh kathna naahin.

Kehna tha so keh diya, ab kuchh kaha na jaaye
Ek raha dooja gaya, dariya leher samaaye.

Acknowledgements

~

Gratitude first and foremost to this folk tradition of oral Kabir, which has kept the words and spirit of Kabir alive in this land for over five hundred years and counting! I'm grateful to be a small part of this vast and wonderful stream.

To Shabnam Virmani, for being the inspiring vehicle which led me into the land of Kabir. Her work, her voice and her sense of joy have been a big blessing in my life.

To Prahlad Singh Tipanya, Mahesha Ram, Kaluram Bamaniya, Parvathy Baul, Mukhtiyar Ali, Mooralala Marwada, and countless other singers who embody and transmit the songs and spirit of Kabir and other mystic poets of this land. They share their songs and their wisdom with very generous hearts.

To Srishti Manipal Institute of Art, Design & Technology, Bengaluru, where I spent several years as part of the Kabir Project, which is generously hosted and supported by Srishti. Some of the material in the present book is an extension of the work done while at the Kabir Project, where I spent some very fulfilling years writing, translating, travelling, documenting, curating, archiving and co-designing this wonderful digital archive known as Ajab Shahar.

To my mom, sister and all my dear friends close to my heart. You know who you are. Your love and support means, and has always meant, a lot. Thank you.

To all the communities and events that have now sprung up around the idea of Kabir, and all the fellow Kabir lovers whom I have met on this path.

To Swati Chopra and HarperCollins India, for believing in this project and giving it such a beautiful form.

To Mita Kapur and Siyahi, Jaipur, for the constant support and encouragement.

And to you, the reader, for letting Kabir speak to your soul.

Notes

1   Apoorvanand, a Professor of Hindi literature at Delhi University, calls it a tradition that the people of India have invented for themselves. To quote: 'Can we say that all these Kabirs are inventions of a collective psyche that have happened over time? And hence to look for an "authentic" Kabir is a futile exercise. In fact, I feel that we can go to the extent of saying that Kabir was not one person, who was born and died somewhere. Kabir doesn't belong to any specific time or age. Kabir is a collective poetic voice that the common folk of India have invented for themselves.' Talk at a Refresher Course on Indian Psychology organized in 2010 by the Department of Psychology, New Delhi: Delhi University. https://www.youtube.com/watch?v=t7a24_EJI6U last accessed on 5 April 2023.

2   See the glossary of W.M. Callewaert's *The Hindi Songs of Namdev,* Peeters Publishers, Leuven, 1989.

3   Per Kvaerne, paraphrased by Linda Hess in *The Bijak of Kabir,* OUP, New Delhi, 2002, p. 138.

4   Hazariprasad Dwivedi, *Kabir,* New Delhi: Rajkamal Prakashan, 1971, p. 67.

5   Kabir scholar Purushottam Agrawal in a talk at a 'Festival of Kabir' organized by the Kabir Project in Bangalore in February 2009, at which I was present. 'My Personal and Political Kabir'. https://www.youtube.com/watch?v=bWyTFl6s62s last accessed on 5 April 2023.

6 'Goraksh Siddhanta Sangrah', cited by Hazariprasad Dwivedi in *Kabir*, Rajkamal Prakashan, p. 72.

7 Compare Patanjali's famous description of yoga as 'citta vritti nirodhah', that is the cessaton of the functions of the mind.

8 This is part of a much larger poem found in many written sources, beginning with 'Allah-Raam jeeu tere naai'. This is the most powerful part of the poem, which has gained an existence of its own.

9 This refers to the popular belief that dying in Varanasi (Kashi) led directly to liberation whereas dying in Maghar resulted in rebirth as an ass.

10 This song uses a series of examples of extreme, unwavering devotion to something. The papeeha bird, the deer, the warrior and the widow. Legend holds that the rain that falls under the 'Swati nakshatra' (the fifteenth house of the moon in the Indian system of astrology) is so auspicious/powerful that it causes pearls to form in shells, and the 'chaatak', a legendary bird, here called 'papeeha' (the hawk-cuckoo or brainfever bird), drinks only of this rain. Also in legend, deer is said to be attracted by music or certain sounds and hunters use this fact to trap them. The widow refers to the now largely abandoned tradition of 'sati', where the widow had the choice, or was coerced, to give up her life on the funeral pyre of her dead husband.

Select Bibliography

〜

Agrawal, Purushottam. *Kabir, Kabir*. Westland, Chennai, 2021.

Das, Abhilash. *Kabir Amrit Vani*. Kabir Parakh Sansthan, Allahabad, 1967.

Das, Abhilash. *Kahat Kabir*. Kabir Parakh Sansthan, Allahabad, 2000.

Das, Shyam Sundar (ed.). *Kabir Granthavali*. Nagari Pracharini Sabha, Varanasi, 1928.

Dharwadkar, Vinay (tr.). *Kabir: The Weaver's Songs*. Penguin Books India, Delhi, 2003.

Dwivedi, Hazariprasad. *Kabir*. Rajkamal Prakashan, New Delhi, 1971.

Ezekiel, Isaac A. *Kabir: The Great Mystic*. Radha Soami Satsang Beas, Dera Baba Jaimal Singh, 1966.

Hess, Linda. *Singing Emptiness*. Seagull Books, Calcutta, 2009.

Hess, Linda, and Shukdeo Singh (tr.). *The Bijak of Kabir*. Oxford University Press, New Delhi, 2002.

Kabir Sahib ka Bijak. Belvedere Press, Allahabad, 1926.

Lorenzen, David. *Kabir Legends and Ananta Das's Kabir Parachai*. State University of New York Press, New York, 1991.

Mehrotra, Arvind Krishna. *Essential Kabir*. Hachette India, Delhi, 2011.

Rikhi, Vipul. *One Palace, A Thousand Doorways*. Speaking Tiger, Delhi, 2019.

Vaudeville, Charlotte. *A Weaver Named Kabir*. Oxford University Press, New Delhi, 1993.

About the Author

~

Vipul Rikhi is a writer, singer, poet, storyteller and translator immersed in the oral traditions of Kabir and other Bhakti and Sufi poets for over a decade. He is the author of several books of poetry, fiction and translation. His most recent books are *One Palace, a Thousand Doorways*, a book of translations, and *I Saw Myself: Journeys with Shah Abdul Latif Bhitai* (co-authored).

Vipul's work with the very well-known Kabir Project has involved writing, translations, research, curations and the creation of a vast digital archive called 'Ajab Shahar'. In the course of these magical journeys, he developed a deep love for singing mystic poetry in the folk music traditions and now performs nationally and internationally. He has a wide following through both his writing and his music.

Website: https://vipulrikhi.com/

30 Years *of*

 HarperCollins *Publishers* India

At HarperCollins, we believe in telling the best stories and finding the widest possible readership for our books in every format possible. We started publishing 30 years ago; a great deal has changed since then, but what has remained constant is the passion with which our authors write their books, the love with which readers receive them, and the sheer joy and excitement that we as publishers feel in being a part of the publishing process.

Over the years, we've had the pleasure of publishing some of the finest writing from the subcontinent and around the world, and some of the biggest bestsellers in India's publishing history. Our books and authors have won a phenomenal range of awards, and we ourselves have been named Publisher of the Year the greatest number of times. But nothing has meant more to us than the fact that millions of people have read the books we published, and somewhere, a book of ours might have made a difference.

As we step into our fourth decade, we go back to that one word – a word which has been a driving force for us all these years.

Read.

Harper
Collins

HARPER
PERENNIAL

HARPER
BUSINESS

HARPER
BLACK

हार्पर
हिन्दी

HarperCollins
Children'sBooks

HARPER
DESIGN

HARPER
VANTAGE

Harper
Sport